Hands-On Microservices with C#

Designing a real-world, enterprise-grade microservice
ecosystem with the efficiency of C# 7

Matt R. Cole

BIRMINGHAM - MUMBAI

Hands-On Microservices with C#

Commissioning Editor: Pavan Ramchandani
Acquisition Editor: Aman Singh
Content Development Editor: Mayur Pawanikar
Technical Editor: Suwarna Patil
Copy Editor: Safis Editing
Project Coordinator: Nidhi Joshi
Proofreader: Safis Editing
Indexer: Mariammal Chettiyar
Graphics: Jason Monterio
Production Coordinator: Nilesh Mohite

First published: June 2018

Production reference: 1290618

Published by Packt Publishing Ltd.
Livery Place
35 Livery Street
Birmingham
B3 2PB, UK.

ISBN 978-1-78953-368-2

www.packtpub.com

`mapt.io`

Mapt is an online digital library that gives you full access to over 5,000 books and videos, as well as industry leading tools to help you plan your personal development and advance your career. For more information, please visit our website.

Why subscribe?

- Spend less time learning and more time coding with practical eBooks and Videos from over 4,000 industry professionals

- Improve your learning with Skill Plans built especially for you

- Get a free eBook or video every month

- Mapt is fully searchable

- Copy and paste, print, and bookmark content

PacktPub.com

Did you know that Packt offers eBook versions of every book published, with PDF and ePub files available? You can upgrade to the eBook version at `www.PacktPub.com` and, as a print book customer, you are entitled to a discount on the eBook copy. Get in touch with us at `service@packtpub.com` for more details.

At `www.PacktPub.com`, you can also read a collection of free technical articles, sign up for a range of free newsletters, and receive exclusive discounts and offers on Packt books and eBooks.

Contributors

About the author

Matt R. Cole is a seasoned developer with 30 years' experience in Microsoft Windows, C, C++, C#, and .NET. He previously wrote a speech and audio VOIP system for NASA for use with the Space Shuttle and a space station. He is the owner of Evolved AI Solutions, a premier provider of advanced ML/Bio-AI technologies. He developed the first enterprise-grade microservice framework (written fully in C# and .NET) used by a major hedge fund in NYC and also developed the first Bio-AI Swarm framework, which fully integrates mirror and canonical neurons.

> *I want to thank my beautiful wife for once again putting up with me authoring another book. Without her help and support, I'd still be on chapter 1...*

About the reviewers

Giuseppe Ciaburro holds a PhD in environmental technical physics and two master's degrees. His research is on machine learning applications in the study of urban sound environments. He works at the Built Environment Control Laboratory, Università degli Studi della Campania Luigi Vanvitelli (Italy). He has over 15 years' experience in programming Python, R, and MATLAB, first in the field of combustion, and then in acoustics and noise control. He has several publications to his credit.

Doug Ortiz is an experienced enterprise Cloud, big data, data analytics, and solutions architect who has designed, developed, re-engineered, and integrated enterprise solutions. His other expertise is in Amazon Web Services, Azure, Google Cloud, business intelligence, Hadoop, Spark, NoSQL databases, and SharePoint, to mention a few.

He is the founder of Illustris, LLC, and can be reached at dougortiz@illustris.org.

> *Huge thanks to my wonderful wife, Milla, as well as Maria, Nikolay, and our children, for all their support.*

Rich Pizzo has many years of experience in the design and development of software and systems. He was a senior architect and project lead, especially in the realm of financial engineering and trading systems. He was the chief technologist at two companies. His knowledge and expertise in digital electronics left its mark in the software domain, as well in providing heterogeneous solutions to tough optimization problems. He has come up with many unique solutions for maximizing computing performance, utilizing Altera FPGAs and the Quartus development environment and test suite.

Packt is searching for authors like you

If you're interested in becoming an author for Packt, please visit authors.packtpub.com and apply today. We have worked with thousands of developers and tech professionals, just like you, to help them share their insight with the global tech community. You can make a general application, apply for a specific hot topic that we are recruiting an author for, or submit your own idea.

Table of Contents

Preface

Welcome to *Hands-On Microservices with C#*. In this book, we will develop a microservice ecosystem that you can immediately put in place in your organization to experience the many benefits of a microservice architecture. No advanced math, no formulas, just straight hands-on development (save a bit of introductory material).

Who this book is for

This book is for the developer learning to see a different implementation of microservices than the typical web page or `Hello World` example. In this book, we will build a real-world microservice ecosystem similar to those I have built for large enterprises. You will have the flexibility to customize every aspect of the process if you so desire.

It is expected that the developer has developed applications before, but no familiarity with microservice architecture is assumed or required. If you have 1-3 years of .NET C# development experience, this book will be a perfect fit for you.

I should note that the microservices within this book, like the book itself, are designed to make your mind open to the many possibilities of a microservice architecture. You can transform any of the microservices into what fits your organization. In fact, this is the goal, that the creative juices will flow and you will turn this ecosystem into something that works best for you.

What this book covers

Chapter 1, *Let's Talk Microservices, Messages, and Tools*, covers all of our introductory material required for the rest of the book.

Chapter 2, *ReflectInsight – Microservice Logging Redefined*, gives a brief overview of ReflectInsight and the rich, powerful logging capabilities it has to offer.

Chapter 3, *Creating a Base Microservice and Interface*, creates a base class and interface we can use throughout the book and all of our microservices. We also discuss base classes, interfaces, and inheritance for those who need a quick refresher.

Chapter 4, *Designing a Memory Management Microservice*, develops a memory management microservice capable of tracing and reporting memory requirements. High CPU, too much RAM, garbage collection, all will be covered in the design. We will also cover why some of these things are important to know in a microservice ecosystem.

Chapter 5, *Designing a Deployment Monitor Microservice*, helps us develop a microservice capable of knowing about and monitoring deployments.

Chapter 6, *Designing a Scheduling Microservice*, develops a microservice that can execute scheduled jobs. While scheduling information is built within this microservice, the reader can open it up to use the messages we have shown thus far and drive the scheduled jobs from there.

Chapter 7, *Designing an Email Microservice*, covers a microservice that can send emails. Exercises are left for the user to expand this microservice to do even more. Separation of concerns is discussed in this chapter as well.

Chapter 8, *Designing a File Monitoring Microservice*, is where we make two microservices that are capable of listening to filesystem events and then posting those events via our messages. This is our first microservice that does not respond to a message but rather sends one when it needs to. The reader is free to expand this microservice to denote the hyperparameters needed to programmatically drive the file monitoring.

Chapter 9, *Creating a Machine Learning Microservice*, implements a CNN contained within a microservice. We will show how to control it asynchronously via messages.

Chapter 10, *Creating a Quantitative Financial Microservice*, develops a quant microservice capable of working with credit default swaps and bonds. This chapter is an exercise for the user to be able to adapt the microservice to their specific needs.

Chapter 11, *Trello Microservice – Board Status Updating*, works with the famous and intuituive Trello service, a Kanban board that is incredibly easy to use. We will show you how the microservice can programmatically add boards, lists, and cards. This can be adapted to Team Foundation Service, Jira, or an other Kanban board application that has a programmatical interface.

Chapter 12, *Microservice Manager – The Nexus*, develops a microservice whose job is to manage all the other microservices in the ecosystem. You will see how important it is to have such a microservice in your ecosystem, from health monitoring to job scheduling and more.

Chapter 13, *Creating a Blockchain Bitcoin Microservice,* implements a small blockchain microservice, and we will spend some of our money here. Cryptocurrency knowledge will not be covered, but it is hoped that again the creative juices will flow.

Chapter 14, *Adding Speech and Search to Your Microservice,* shows you how to add text-to-speech to your application. We will do this both in terms of speaking text, and also searching Wikipedia for results and then speaking those results aloud.

Appendix A, *Best Practices,* discusses best practices for designing and using your *Microservice* ecosystem.

To get the most out of this book

1. The reader should be a C# .NET developer with at least 1 year of developing applications. The reader should also be familiar with Microsoft Visual Studio.
2. The reader should have the latest .NET framework installed on their machine as well as the latest version of Microsoft Visual Studio. The community version of Microsoft Visual Studio will accomplish both.

Download the example code files

You can download the example code files for this book from your account at www.packtpub.com. If you purchased this book elsewhere, you can visit www.packtpub.com/support and register to have the files emailed directly to you.

You can download the code files by following these steps:

1. Log in or register at www.packtpub.com.
2. Select the **SUPPORT** tab.
3. Click on **Code Downloads & Errata**.
4. Enter the name of the book in the **Search** box and follow the onscreen instructions.

Once the file is downloaded, please make sure that you unzip or extract the folder using the latest version of:

- WinRAR/7-Zip for Windows
- Zipeg/iZip/UnRarX for Mac
- 7-Zip/PeaZip for Linux

The code bundle for the book is also hosted on GitHub at `https://github.com/PacktPublishing/Hands-On-Microservices-with-CSharp`. In case there's an update to the code, it will be updated on the existing GitHub repository.

We also have other code bundles from our rich catalog of books and videos available at `https://github.com/PacktPublishing/`. Check them out!

Download the color images

We also provide a PDF file that has color images of the screenshots/diagrams used in this book. You can download it here: `https://www.packtpub.com/sites/default/files/downloads/HandsOnMicroserviceswithCSharp_ColorImages.pdf`.

Conventions used

There are a number of text conventions used throughout this book.

`CodeInText`: Indicates code words in text, database table names, folder names, filenames, file extensions, pathnames, dummy URLs, user input, and Twitter handles. Here is an example: "Mount the downloaded `WebStorm-10*.dmg` disk image file as another disk in your system."

A block of code is set as follows:

```
 public class DeploymentStartMessage
 {
 public DateTime Date { get; set; }
 }
 public class DeploymentStopMessage
 {
 public DateTime Date { get; set; }
 }
```

When we wish to draw your attention to a particular part of a code block, the relevant lines or items are set in bold:

```
bus.Subscribe<MyMessage>("my_subscription_id", msg =>
Console.WriteLine(msg.Text));
```

Bold: Indicates a new term, an important word, or words that you see onscreen. For example, words in menus or dialog boxes appear in the text like this. Here is an example: "A **binding** is a link that you set up to bind a queue to an exchange."

 Warnings or important notes appear like this.

 Tips and tricks appear like this.

Get in touch

Feedback from our readers is always welcome.

General feedback: Email feedback@packtpub.com and mention the book title in the subject of your message. If you have questions about any aspect of this book, please email us at questions@packtpub.com.

Errata: Although we have taken every care to ensure the accuracy of our content, mistakes do happen. If you have found a mistake in this book, we would be grateful if you would report this to us. Please visit www.packtpub.com/submit-errata, selecting your book, clicking on the Errata Submission Form link, and entering the details.

Piracy: If you come across any illegal copies of our works in any form on the Internet, we would be grateful if you would provide us with the location address or website name. Please contact us at copyright@packtpub.com with a link to the material.

If you are interested in becoming an author: If there is a topic that you have expertise in and you are interested in either writing or contributing to a book, please visit authors.packtpub.com.

Reviews

Please leave a review. Once you have read and used this book, why not leave a review on the site that you purchased it from? Potential readers can then see and use your unbiased opinion to make purchase decisions, we at Packt can understand what you think about our products, and our authors can see your feedback on their book. Thank you!

For more information about Packt, please visit `packtpub.com`.

Let's Talk Microservices, Messages, and Tools

1

Microservices are all the rage. They are talked about everywhere, and it seems like everyone wants them nowadays. There are probably as many implementations of them as there are words in this paragraph, and we'll add yet another one into the mix. But this comes from several implementations and years of experience developing enterprise grade microservice ecosystems for big clients. Now, I'm letting you in on the same techniques and best practices I've been using in the real world. And thus, you have the logic behind this book. I'm going to show you how to develop a powerful, flexible, and scalable microservice ecosystem, and hopefully along the way spark ideas for you to go off on your own endeavors and create even more. And we're not talking about some skimpy little web page or a single service; I've packed this book full of more microservices than you can shake a stick at, and I am sure your ideas will take shape and you will enhance this ecosystem to meet your needs.

In this chapter, we will cover:

- What a microservice is
- What a microservice architecture is
- Pros and cons of a microservice
- Installing and an overview of Topshelf
- Installing and an overview of RabbitMQ
- Installing and an overview of EasyNetQ
- Installing and an overview of Autofac
- Installing and an overview of Quartz
- Installing and an overview of Noda Time

What is a microservice?

Ok, let's just go ahead and get this one out of the way. Let's start this book off by talking a bit about exactly what a microservice is, to us at least. Let's start with a simplistic visual diagram of what we're going to accomplish in this book. This diagram says it all, and if this looks too confusing, this might be a good place to stop reading!

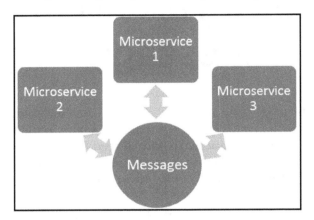

Let's next agree to define a microservice as an independently deployable and developable, small, modular service that addresses a specific and unique business process or problem, and communicates via a lightweight event-based, asynchronous, message-based architecture. A lot of words in that one I know, but I promise by this end of the book that the approach will make perfect sense to you. Basically, what we are talking about here is the **Messages** central component in the previous diagram.

I know that some of you might be asking yourselves, what's the difference between a service and a microservice? That is one very good question. Lord knows I've had some very heated discussions from non-believers over the years, and no doubt you might as well. So, let's talk a bit about what a **Service-Oriented Architecture (SOA)** is.

Service-Oriented Architecture

The SOA is a software design paradigm where services are the central focus. For the purposes of discussion and clarity, let's define a service as a discrete unit of functionality that can be accessed remotely and acted upon independently. The characteristics of a service in terms of a SOA are:

- It represents a specific business function or purpose (hopefully)
- It is self-contained
- It can and should function as a black box
- It may also be comprised of other associated services
- There is a hard and dedicated contract for each service (usually)

Some folks like to consider a microservice nothing more than a more formalized and refined version of an SOA. Perhaps in some ways, that could be the case. Many people believe that the SOA just never really formalized, and microservices are the missing formality. And although I am sure an argument could be made for that being true, microservices are usually designed differently, with a response-actor paradigm, and they usually use smaller or siloed databases (when permissible), and smaller and faster messaging protocols versus things like a giant **Enterprise Service Bus** (**ESB**).

Let's take a moment and talk about the microservice architecture itself.

Microservice architecture

Just as there is no one set definition for a microservice, there is also not one set architecture. What we will do is make a list of some of the characteristics that we view a microservice architecture to have. That list would then look something like this:

- Each microservice can be deployed, developed, maintained, and then redeployed independently.
- Each microservice focuses on a specific business purpose and goal and is non-monolithic.
- Each microservice receives requests, processes them, and then may or may not send a response.

- Microservices practice decentralized governance and in some cases, when permissible, decentralized data management.
- Perhaps most importantly, at least in my mind anyways, I always design a microservice around failure. In fact, they are designed to fail. By following this paradigm, you will always be able to handle failures gracefully and not allow one failing microservice to negatively impact the entire ecosystem. By negatively impact, I mean a state where all other microservices are throwing exceptions due to the one errant microservice. Every microservice needs to be able to gracefully handle not being able to complete its task.
- Finally, let's stay flexible and state that our microservice architecture is free to remain fluid and evolutionary.
- No microservice talks directly to another microservice. Communication is always done in the form of messages.

With all that in mind, we've now created our definition of a microservice and its architecture and characteristics. Feel free to adjust these as you or your situation sees fit. Remember, as C# developers we don't always have the luxury, save truly greenfield projects, to dictate all the terms. Do the best you can with the room you have to operate within. As an example, chances are you will have to work with the corporate database and their rules rather than a small siloed database as described earlier. It's still a microservice, so go for it!

Pros and cons

Let's run down some pros and cons of a microservice architecture.

Pros

Here are a few of the positive points of a microservice architecture:

- They give developers the freedom to independently architect, develop, and deploy services
- Microservices can be developed in different languages if permitted
- Easier integration and deployment than traditional monolithic applications and services

- Microservices are organized around specific business capabilities
- When change is required, only the specific microservice needs to be changed and redeployed
- Enhanced fault isolation
- They are easier to scale
- Integration to external services is made easier

Cons

Here are a few negatives when considering a microservice architecture. Please keep in mind that negative does not equal bad, just information that may affect your decision:

- Testing can be more involved
- Duplication of effort and code can occur more often
- Product management could become more complicated
- Developers may have more work when it comes to communications infrastructure
- Memory consumption may increase

Case study

Let's take a look at someone who took a monolithic application and broke it down into components and created a microservice-based system. The following is the story of Parkster; I think you will enjoy it!

A growing digital parking service from Sweden is right now breaking down their monolithic application towards microservices. Follow their story!

Portable parking meter in your pocket

Founded in 2010, Parkster has quickly become one of the fastest growing digital parking services in Sweden. Their vision is to make it quick and easy for you to pay your parking fees with your smartphone, via your Parkster app, SMS, or voicemail. They want to see a world where you don't need to guesstimate the required parking time or stand in line waiting by a busy parking meter. It should be easy to pay for parking—for everyone, everywhere. Moreover, Parkster doesn't want the customer to pay more when using tools of the future— that's why there are no extra fees if you are using Parkster's app when parking:

Breaking up a tightly coupled monolithic application

Like many other companies, Parkster started out with a monolithic architecture. They wanted to have their business model proven before they went further. A monolithic application is where the whole application is built as a single unit. All code for a system is in a single codebase that is compiled together and produces a single system.

Having one codebase seemed the easiest and quickest solution at the time, and solved their core business problems, which included connecting devices with people, parking zones, billing, and payments. A few years later, they decided to break up the monolith into multiple small codebases, which they did through multiple microservices communicating via message queues.

Parkster tried out their parking service for the first time in Lund, Sweden. After that, they rapidly expanded into more cities and introduced new features. The core model grew, and components became tightly coupled:

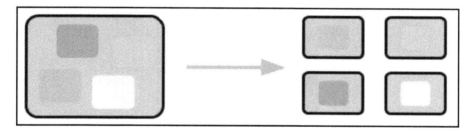

Deploying the codebase meant deploying everything at once. One big codebase made it hard and difficult to fix bugs and to add new features. A deep knowledge was also required before making an attempt at a single small code change; no one wants to add new code that could disrupt operations in some unforeseen way. One day they had enough—the application had to be decoupled. *The biggest reason we moved from monolith to microservice were decoupling.*

Application decoupling

Parkster's move from a monolith architecture to a microservice architecture is a working progress. They are breaking up their software into a collection of small, isolated services, where each service can independently deploy and scale as needed, independently of other services. Their system today has about 15-20 microservices, where the core app is written in Java.

They are already enjoying their changes: *It's very nice to focus on a specific limited part of the system instead of having to think about the entire system, every time you do something new or make changes. As we grow, I think we will benefit even more from this change.* said Anders Davoust, developer at Parkster:

Breaking down their codebase has also given the software developers the freedom to use whatever technologies make sense for a particular service. Different parts of the application can evolve independently, be it written in different languages and/or be maintained by separated developer teams. For example, one part of the system uses MongoDB and another part uses MySQL. Most code is written in Java, but parts of the system are written in Clojure. Parkster is using the open source system Kubernetes as a container orchestration platform.

Resiliency—the capacity to recover quickly from difficulties

Applications might be delayed or crash sometimes; it happens. It could be due to timeouts or that you simply have errors in your code that could affect the whole application.

Another thing Parkster really like about their system today is that it can still be operational, even if part of the backend processing is delayed or broken. Everything will not break just because one small part of the system is not operating as it should. By breaking up the system into autonomous components, Parkster inherently created more resiliency.

Message queues, RabbitMQ, and CloudAMQP

Parkster is separating different components via message queues. A message queue may force the receiving application to confirm that it has completed a task and that it is safe to remove the task from the queue. The message will just stay in the queue if anything fails in the receiving application. A message queue provides temporary message storage when the destination program is busy or not connected.

The message broker used between all microservices in Parkster is RabbitMQ. *It was a simple choice - we had used RabbitMQ in other projects before we built Parkster and we had a good experience of RabbitMQ.* The reason they went for CloudAMQP, a hosted RabbitMQ solution, was because they felt that CloudAMQP had way more knowledge about management of RabbitMQ than they had. They simply wanted to put their focus on the product instead of spending days configuring and handling server setups. CloudAMQP has been at the forefront when it comes to RabbitMQ server configurations and optimization since 2012.

I asked what they like about CloudAMQP, and I received a quick answer: *I love the support that CloudAMQP gives us, always quick feedback and good help.*

Now, Parkster's goal is to get rid of the old monolithic repo entirely, and focus on a new era where the whole system is built upon microservices.

Messaging concepts

The following is a list of concepts that relate to messaging:

- **Producer**: Application that sends the messages.
- **Consumer**: Application that receives the messages.
- **Queue**: Buffer that stores messages.
- **Message**: Information that is sent from the producer to a consumer through RabbitMQ.
- **Connection**: A connection is a TCP connection between your application and the RabbitMQ broker.
- **Channel**: A channel is a virtual connection inside a connection. When you are publishing or consuming messages from a queue - it's all done over a channel.
- **Exchange**: Receives messages from producers and pushes them to queues depending on rules defined by the exchange type. In order to receive messages, a queue needs to be bound to at least one exchange.
- **Binding**: A binding is a link between a queue and an exchange.
- **Routing key**: The routing key is a key that the exchange looks at to decide how to route the message to queues. The routing key is like an *address* for the message.
- **Advanced Message Queuing Protocol (AMQP)**: AMQP is the protocol used by RabbitMQ for messaging.
- **Users**: It is possible to connect to RabbitMQ with a given username and password. Every user can be assigned permissions such as rights to read, write, and configure privileges within the instance. Users can also be assigned permissions to specific virtual hosts.
- **Vhost**: A virtual host provides a way to segregate applications using the same RabbitMQ instance. Different users can have different access privileges to different vhosts and queues, and exchanges can be created so they only exist in one vhost.

Message queues

Throughout this book, we will be dealing a lot with message queues. You will also see it prevalent in the software we are developing. Messaging queues are how our ecosystem communicates, maintains separation of concerns, and allows for fluid and fast development. With that being said, before we get too far along into something else, let's spend some time discussing exactly what message queues are and what they do.

Let's think about the functionality of a message queue. They are two sided components; messages enter from one side and exit from the other one. Thus, each message queue can establish connections on both sides; on the input side, a queue fetches messages from **one** or more exchanges, while on the output side, the queue can be connected to one or more consumers. From the single queue point of view being connected to more than one exchange with the same routing key, this is transparent, since the only thing that concerns the message queue itself are the incoming messages:

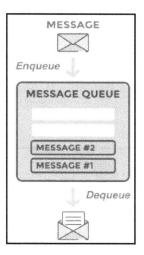

Put another way...

The basic architecture of a message queue is simple. There are client applications called **producers** that create messages and deliver them to the broker (the message queue). Other applications, called **consumers**, connect to the queue and subscribe to the messages to be processed. A software can be a producer, or consumer, or both a consumer and a producer of messages. Messages placed onto the queue are stored until the consumer retrieves them:

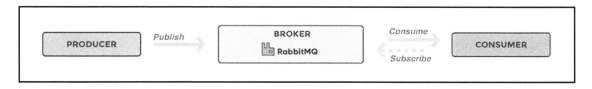

And, breaking that down even further:

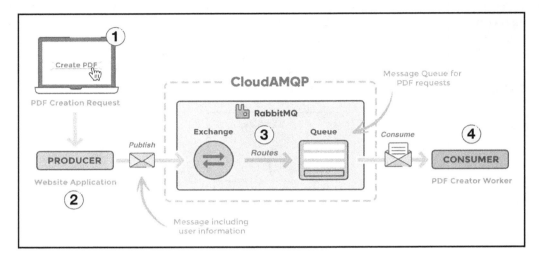

The preceding diagram illustrates the following process:

1. The user sends a PDF creation request to the web application
2. The web application (the producer) sends a message to RabbitMQ, including data from the request, such as name and email
3. An exchange accepts the messages from a producer application and routes them to correct message queues for PDF creation
4. The PDF processing worker (the consumer) receives the task and starts the processing of the PDF

Let's now look at some of the different message queue configurations that we can use. For now, let's think of a queue as an ordered collection or list of messages. In the diagrams that follow, we're going to use **P** to represent a producer, **C** to represent a consumer, and the red rectangles to represent a queue.

Here's our legend:

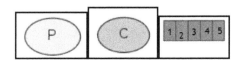

Producer consumer queue

Let's start by taking the simplest of all possible scenarios. We have a single producer, which sends one or more messages (each message is one red block) to a single consumer, such as in the following:

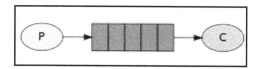

Our next step up the difficulty ladder would be to have a single producer publish one or more messages to multiple consumers, such as in the following diagram. This is distributing tasks (work) among different workers, also sometimes referred to as the competing consumers pattern. This means that each consumer will take one or more messages. Depending upon how the message queues are set up, the consumers may each receive a copy of every message, or alternate in their reception based upon availability. So, in one scenario, consumer one may take ten messages, consumer two may take five, then consumer one takes another ten. Alternatively, the messages that consumer one takes, consumer two does not get and vice versa:

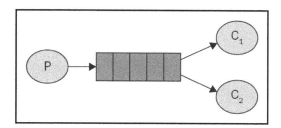

Next, we have the ever so famous publish/subscribe paradigm, where messages are sent to various consumers at once. Each consumer will get a copy of the message, unlike the scenario shown previously where consumers may have to compete for each message:

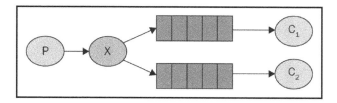

Our next scenario provides us with the ability for a client to selectively decide which message(s) they are interested in, and only receive those. Using a direct exchange, the consumers are able to ask for the type of message that they wish to receive:

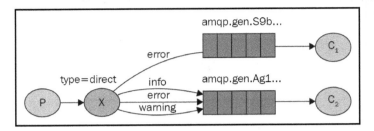

If we were to expand this direct exchange map out a little bit, here's what our system might look like:

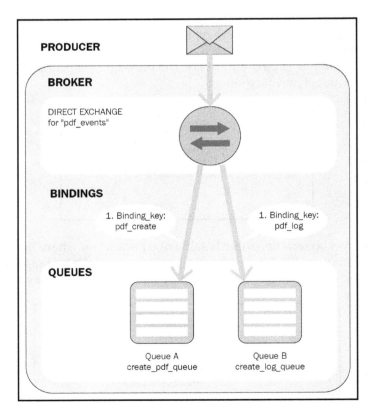

A direct exchange delivers messages to queues based on a message routing key. The routing key is a message attribute added into the message header by the producer. The routing key can be seen as an address that the exchange is using to decide how to route the message. A message goes to the queue(s) whose binding key exactly matches the routing key of the message.

The direct exchange type is useful when you would like to distinguish between messages published to the same exchange using a simple string identifier.

Next, as you will see me use quite heavily in this book, our consumers can receive selected messages based upon patterns (topics) with what is known as a **topic queue**. Users subscribe to the topic(s) that they wish to receive, and those messages will be sent to them. Note that this is not a competing consumers pattern where only one microservice will receive the message. Any microservice that is subscribed will receive the selected messages:

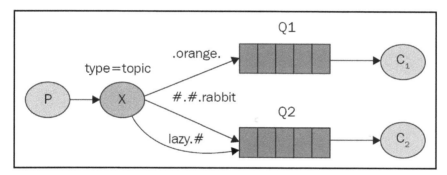

If we expand this one out a little bit, we can see what our system might look like:

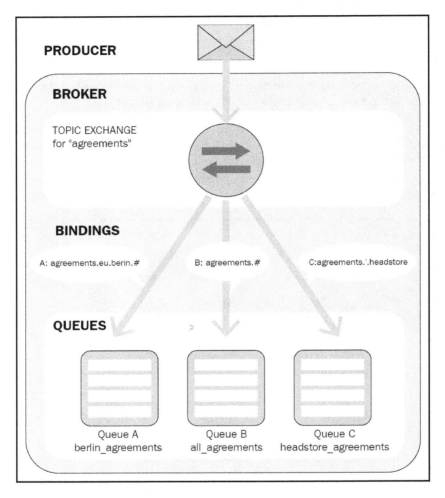

The topic exchanges route messages to queues based on wildcard matches between the routing key and routing pattern specified by the queue binding. Messages are routed to one or many queues based on a matching between a message routing key and this pattern. The routing key must be a list of words, delimited by a period (.). The routing patterns may contain an asterisk (*) to match a word in a specific position of the routing key (for example, a routing pattern of **agreements.*.*.b.*** will only match routing keys where the first word is **agreements** and the fourth word is *b*). A pound symbol (#) indicates a match on zero or more words (for example, a routing pattern of **agreements.eu.berlin.#** matches any routing keys beginning with **agreements.eu.berlin**).

The consumers indicate which topics they are interested in (such as subscribing to a feed for an individual tag). The consumer creates a queue and sets up a binding with a given routing pattern to the exchange. All messages with a routing key that match the routing pattern will be routed to the queue and stay there until the consumer consumes the message.

Finally, we have the request/reply pattern. This scenario will have a client subscribing to a message, but rather than consume the message and end there, a reply message is required, usually containing the status result of the operation that took place. The loop and chain of custody is not complete until the final response is received and acknowledged:

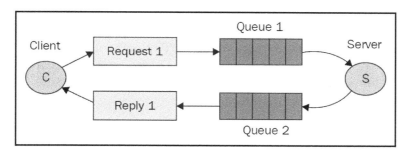

Now that you know all you need to know about message queues and how they work, let's fill in our initial visual diagram a bit more so it's a bit more reflective of what we are doing, what we hope to accomplish, and how we expect our ecosystem to function. Although we will primarily be focusing on topic exchanges, we may occasionally switch to fanouts, direct, and others. In the end, the visual that we are after for our ecosystem is this:

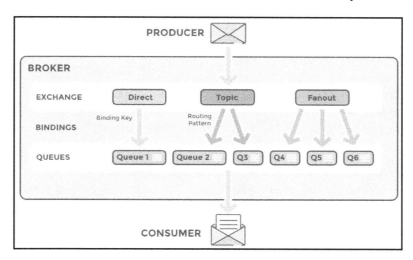

Creating common messages

Let's start with a very simple message, the deployment messages:

```
public class DeploymentStartMessage
{
public DateTime Date { get; set; }
}
public class DeploymentStopMessage
{
public DateTime Date { get; set; }
}
```

As you can see, they are not overly complicated. What will happen is that we will have a `DeploymentMonitor` microservice. As soon as our deployment kicks off, we will send a `DeploymentStartMessage` to the message queue. Our microservice manager will receive the message, and immediately disable tracking each microservice's health until the `DeploymentStopMessage` is received.

 Always include all your messages in the same namespace. This makes it much easier for EasyNetQ and its type name resolver to know where the messages are coming from. It also gives you a centralized location for all your messages, and lastly, prevents a lot of weird looking exchange and queue names!

Message subscriptions

Now that we have shown you what a deployment message looks like, let's discuss what happens when you subscribe to a message.

An EasyNetQ subscriber subscribes to a message type (the .NET type of the message class). Once the subscription to a type has been set up by calling the `Subscribe` method, a persistent queue will be created on the RabbitMQ broker and any messages of that type will be placed on the queue. RabbitMQ will send any messages from the queue to the subscriber whenever it is connected.

To subscribe to a message, we need to give EasyNetQ an action to perform whenever a message arrives. We do this by passing the `Subscribe` method a delegate such as this:

```
bus.Subscribe<MyMessage>("my_subscription_id", msg =>
Console.WriteLine(msg.Text));
```

Now, every time an instance of `MyMessage` is published, EasyNetQ will call our delegate and print the message's `Text` property to the console.

The subscription ID that you pass to subscribe is important

EasyNetQ will create a unique queue on the RabbitMQ broker for each unique combination of message type and subscription ID. Each call to Subscribe creates a new queue consumer. If you call the `Subscribe` method two times with the same message type and subscription ID, you will create two consumers consuming from the same queue. RabbitMQ will then round-robin successive messages to each consumer in turn. This is great for scaling and work-sharing. Say you've created a service that processes a particular message, but it's getting overloaded with work. Simply start a new instance of that service (on the same machine, or a different one) and without having to configure anything, you get automatic scaling.

If you call the `Subscribe` method two times with different subscription IDs but the same message type, you will create two queues, each with its own consumer. A copy of each message of the given type will be routed to each queue, so each consumer will get all the messages (of that type). This is great if you've got several different services that all care about the same message type.

Considerations when writing the subscribe callback delegate

As messages are received from queues subscribed to via EasyNetQ, they are placed on an in-memory queue. A single thread sits in a loop taking messages from the queue and calling their action delegates. Since the delegates are processed one at a time on a single thread, you should avoid long-running synchronous IO operations. Return control from the delegate as soon as possible.

Using SubscribeAsync

`SubscribeAsync` allows your subscriber delegate to return a `Task` immediately and then asynchronously execute long-running IO operations. Once the long-running subscription is complete, simply complete the `Task`.

Canceling subscriptions

All the subscribe methods return an `ISubscriptionResult`. It contains properties that describe the `IExchange` and `IQueue` used by the underlying `IConsumer`; these can be further manipulated using the advanced API `IAdvancedBus` if required.

You can cancel a subscriber at any time by calling `Dispose` on the `ISubscriptionResult` instance or on its `ConsumerCancellation` property:

```
var subscriptionResult = bus.Subscribe<MyMessage>("sub_id", MyHandler);
subscriptionResult.Dispose();
```

This will stop EasyNetQ consuming from the queue and close the consumer's channel. It is the equivalent to calling `subscriptionResult.ConsumerCancellation.Dispose();`

Note that disposing of the `IBus` or `IAdvancedBus` instance will also cancel all consumers and close the connection to RabbitMQ.

Versioning messages

Even though I can honestly say that I have developed interfaces that could accommodate any change made to both sides without ever modifying the interface, most people don't design to that extreme. There will, more likely than not, come a time where you will have to change a message to accommodate a new feature or request, and so on. Now, we get into the issue of message versioning.

To enable support for versioned messages, we need to ensure the required components are configured. The simplest way to achieve this is as follows:

```
var bus = RabbitHutch.CreateBus( "host=localhost", services =>
services.EnableMessageVersioning() )
```

Once support for versioned messages is enabled, we must explicitly opt-in any messages we want to be treated as versioned. So as an example, let's say we have a message defined called `MyMessage`. As you can see in the following message, it is not versioned and all versions will be treated the same way as any other when it is published:

```
public class MyMessage
{
public string Text { get; set; }
}
```

The next message that you see will be versioned, and ultimately it will find its way to both the V2 and previous subscribers by using the ISupersede interface:

```
public class MyMessageV2 : MyMessage, ISupersede<MyMessage>
{
public int Number { get; set; }
}
```

How does message versioning work?

Let's stop for a second and think about what's happening here. When we publish a message, EasyNetQ usually creates an exchange for the message type and publishes the message to that exchange:

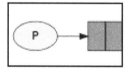

Subscribers create queues that are bound to the exchange and therefore receive any messages published to it:

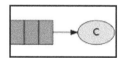

With message versioning enabled, EasyNetQ will create an exchange for each message type in the version hierarchy and bind those exchanges together. When you publish the MyMessageV2 message, it will be sent to the MyMessageV2 exchange, which will automatically forward it to the MyMessage exchange.

When messages are serialized, EasyNetQ stores the message type name in the type property of the message properties. This metadata is sent along with your message to any subscribers, who can then use it to deserialize the message.

With message versioning enabled, EasyNetQ will also store all the superseded message types in a header in the message properties. Subscribers will use this to find the first available type that the message can be deserialized into, meaning that even if an endpoint does not have the latest version of a message, so long as it has a version, it can be deserialized and handled.

Message versioning guidance

Here are a few tips for message versioning:

- If the change cannot be implemented by extending the original message type, then it is not a new version of the message; it is a new message type
- If you are unsure, prefer to create a new message type rather than version an existing message
- Versioned messages should not be used with request/response as the message types are part of the request/response contract and `Request<V1, Response>` is not the same as `Request<V2, Response>`, even if V2 extends V1 (that is, public class `V2 : V1 {}`)
- Versioned messages should not be used with send/receive as this is targeted sending and therefore there is a declared dependency between the sender and the receiver

Message publishing

Messages are not published directly to any specific message queue. Instead, the producer sends messages to an exchange. Exchanges are message routing agents, defined per virtual host within RabbitMQ. An exchange is responsible for the routing of the messages to the different queues. An exchange accepts messages from the producer application and routes them to message queues with the help of header attributes, bindings, and routing keys.

A **binding** is a link that you set up to bind a queue to an exchange.

The **routing key** is a message attribute. The exchange might look at this key when deciding how to route the message to queues (depending on exchange type).

Exchanges, connections, and queues can be configured with parameters such as *durable*, temporary, and auto delete upon creation. Durable exchanges will survive server restarts and will last until they are explicitly deleted. Temporary exchanges exist until RabbitMQ is shut down. Auto-deleted exchanges are removed once the last bound object is unbound from the exchange.

As we begin to explore more about messages, I want to give a big shoutout to Lovisa Johansson at CloudAMQP for permission to reprint information she and others have done an excellent job at obtaining. Everyone should visit CloudAMQP; it is an infinite source of wisdom when it comes to RabbitMQ.

Message flow

The following is a standardly configured RabbitMQ message flow:

1. The producer publishes a message to the exchange.
2. The exchange receives the message and is now responsible for the routing of the message.
3. A binding has to be set up between the queue and the exchange. In this case, we have bindings to two different queues from the exchange. The exchange routes the message in to the queues.
4. The messages stay in the queue until they are handled by a consumer.
5. The consumer handles the message:

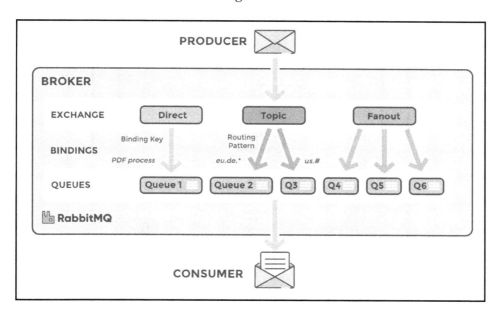

Exchanges

Messages are not published directly to a queue; instead, the producer sends messages to an exchange. An exchange is responsible for the routing of the messages to the different queues. An exchange accepts messages from the producer application and routes them to message queues with the help of bindings and routing keys. A binding is a link between a queue and an exchange:

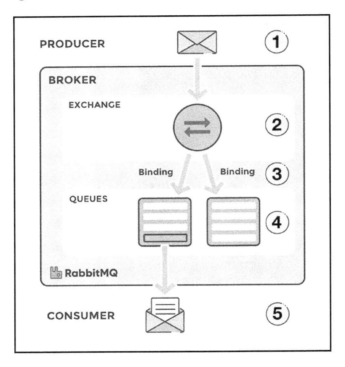

Message flow in RabbitMQ

1. The producer publishes a message to an exchange. When you create the exchange, you have to specify the type of it. The different types of exchanges are explained in detail later on.
2. The exchange receives the message and is now responsible for the routing of the message. The exchange takes different message attributes into account, such as routing key, depending on the exchange type.

3. Bindings have to be created from the exchange to queues. In this case, we see two bindings to two different queues from the exchange. The exchange routes the message into the queues depending on message attributes.

4. The messages stay in the queue until they are handled by a consumer.

5. The consumer handles the message.

Direct exchange

A direct exchange delivers messages to queues based on a message routing key. The routing key can be seen as an address that the exchange is using to decide how to route the message. A message goes to the queues whose binding key exactly matches the routing key of the message.

The direct exchange type is useful when you would like to distinguish messages published to the same exchange using a simple string identifier.

Imagine that **Queue A (create_pdf_queue)** in the following diagram is bound to a direct exchange (**pdf_events**) with the binding key **pdf_create**. When a new message with the routing key **pdf_create** arrives at the direct exchange, the exchange routes it to the queue where the **binding_key = routing_key** is, in this case, to **Queue A (create_pdf_queue)**.

SCENARIO 1:

- **Exchange: pdf_events**
- **Queue A: create_pdf_queue**
- Binding a key between exchange (**pdf_events**) and **Queue A (create_pdf_queue)**: **pdf_create**

SCENARIO 2:

- **Exchange: pdf_events**
- **Queue B: pdf_log_queue**
- Binding a key between exchange (**pdf_events**) and **Queue B (pdf_log_queue)**: **pdf_log**

EXAMPLE:

A message with the routing key **pdf_logis** sent to the exchange **pdf_events**. The message is routed to **pdf_log_queue** because the routing key (**pdf_log**) matches the binding key (**pdf_log**). If the message routing key does not match any binding key, the message will be discarded, as seen in the direct exchange diagram:

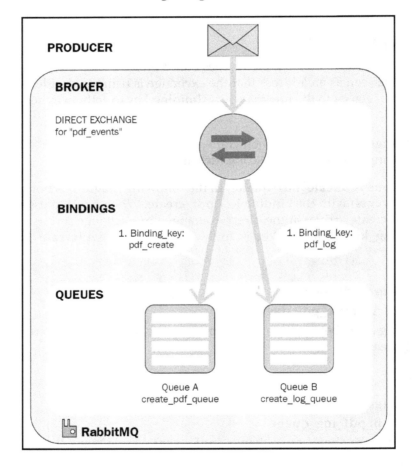

A message goes to the queues whose binding key exactly matches the routing key of the message.

Default exchange

The default exchange is a pre-declared direct exchange with no name, usually referred to by the empty string "". When you use the default exchange, your message will be delivered to the queue with a name equal to the routing key of the message. Every queue is automatically bound to the default exchange with a routing key that is the same as the queue name.

Topic exchange

Topic exchanges route messages to queues based on wildcard matches between the routing key and something called the **routing pattern** specified by the queue binding. Messages are routed to one or many queues based on a matching between a message routing key and this pattern.

The routing key must be a list of words, delimited by a period (.); examples are **agreements.us** and **agreements.eu.stockholm**, which, in this case, identifies agreements that are set up for a company with offices in lots of different locations. The routing patterns may contain an asterisk (*) to match a word in a specific position of the routing key (for example, a routing pattern of **agreements.*.*.b.*** will only match routing keys where the first word is **agreements** and the fourth word is b). A pound symbol (#) indicates a match on zero or more words (for example, a routing pattern of **agreements.eu.berlin.#** matches any routing keys beginning with **agreements.eu.berlin**).

The consumers indicate which topics they are interested in (such as subscribing to a feed for an individual tag). The consumer creates a queue and sets up a binding with a given routing pattern to the exchange. All messages with a routing key that match the routing pattern will be routed to the queue and stay there until the consumer consumes the message.

The following diagram shows three example scenarios:

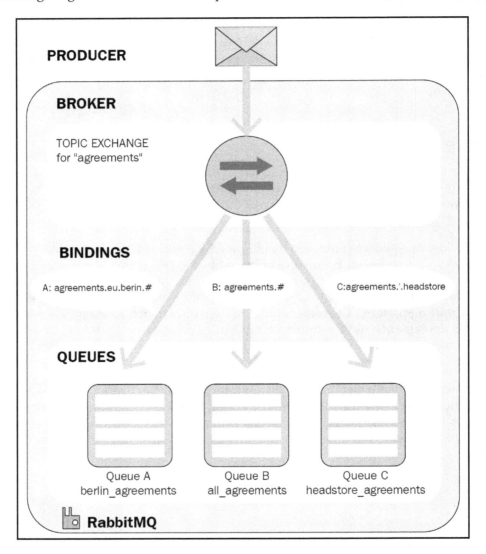

SCENARIO 1:

Consumer A is interested in all the agreements in Berlin:

- **Exchange**: **agreements**
- **Queue A**: **berlin_agreements**

- Routing pattern between exchange (**agreements**) and **Queue A** (**berlin_agreements**): **agreements.eu.berlin.#**
- Example of message routing key that will match: **agreements.eu.berlin** and **agreements.eu.berlin.headstore**

SCENARIO 2:

Consumer B is interested in all the agreements:

- **Exchange: agreements**
- **Queue B: all_agreements**
- Routing pattern between exchange (**agreements**) and **Queue B** (**all_agreements**): **agreements.#**
- Example of message routing key that will match: **agreements.eu.berlin** and **agreements.us**

Topic Exchange: Messages are routed to one or many queues based on a matching between a message routing key and the routing pattern.

SCENARIO 3:

Consumer C is interested in all agreements for European head stores:

- **Exchange: agreements**
- **Queue C: headstore_agreements**
- Routing pattern between exchange (**agreements**) and **Queue C** (**headstore_agreements**): **agreements.eu.*.headstore**
- Example of message routing keys that will match: **agreements.eu.berlin.headstore** and **agreements.eu.stockholm.headstore**

Fanout exchange

The fanout copies and routes a received message to all queues that are bound to it regardless of routing keys or pattern matching, as with direct and topic exchanges. Keys provided will simply be ignored.

Fanout exchanges can be useful when the same message needs to be sent to one or more queues with consumers who may process the same message in different ways.

The fanout copies and routes a received message to all queues that are bound to it regardless of routing keys or pattern matching as with direct and topic exchanges. Keys provided will simply be ignored.

Fanout exchanges can be useful when the same message needs to be sent to one or more queues with consumers who may process the same message in different ways.

The following fanout exchange figure shows an example where a message received by the exchange is copied and routed to all three queues that are bound to the exchange. It could be sport or weather news updates that should be sent out to each connected mobile device when something happens.

The default exchange AMQP brokers must provide for the topic exchange is **amq.fanout**:

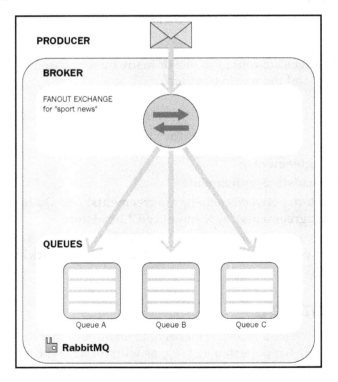

Received messages are routed to all queues that are bound to the exchange.

SCENARIO 1:

- **Exchange**: **sport news**
- **Queue A**: Mobile client **Queue A**
- **Binding**: Binging between the exchange (**sport news**) and **Queue A** (mobile client **Queue A**)

EXAMPLE:

A message is sent to the exchange **sport news**. The message is routed to all queues (**Queue A**, **Queue B**, and **Queue C**) because all queues are bound to the exchange. Provided routing keys are ignored.

Headers exchange

Headers exchange routes are based on arguments containing headers and optional values. Headers exchanges are very similar to topic exchanges, but they route based on header values instead of routing keys. A message is considered matching if the value of the header equals the value specified upon binding.

A special argument named **x-match**, which can be added in the binding between your exchange and your queue, tells if all headers must match or just one. Either any common header between the message and the binding counts as a match, or all the headers referenced in the binding need to be present in the message for it to match. The **x-match** property can have two different values: **any** or **all**, where **all** is the default value. A value of **all** means all header pairs (key, value) must match and a value of **any** means at least one of the header pairs must match. Headers can be constructed using a wider range of data types—integer or hash, for example, instead of a string. The header's exchange type (used with binding argument **any**) is useful for directing messages that may contain a subset of known (unordered) criteria:

- **Exchange**: Binding to **Queue A** with arguments (**key = value**): **format = pdf, type = report, x-match = all**
- **Exchange**: Binding to **Queue B** with arguments (**key = value**): **format = pdf, type = log, x-match = any**
- **Exchange**: Binding to **Queue C** with arguments (**key = value**): **format = zip, type = report, x-match = all**

SCENARIO 1:

Message 1 is published to the exchange with the header arguments **(key = value): format = pdf, type = report** and with the binding argument **x-match = all**.

Message 1 is delivered to **Queue A** —all key/value pair match.

SCENARIO 2:

Message 2 is published to the exchange with header arguments of **(key = value): format = pdf** and with the binding argument **x-match = any**.

Message 2 is delivered to **Queue A** and **Queue B**—the queue is configured to match any of the headers (format or log):

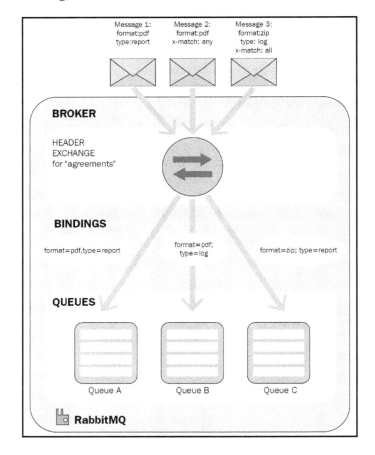

Headers exchange route messages to queues that are bound using arguments (key and value) that contain headers and optional values.

SCENARIO 3:

Message 3 is published to the exchange with the header arguments of (**key = value**): **format = zip, type = log** and with the binding argument **x-match = all**.

Message 3 is not delivered to any queue; the queue is configured to match all of the headers (format or log).

Common messages

Following are all the common messages we have defined for this book. You may feel free to change any one you need to as they are merely guides for you to start thinking in the microservice mindset:

```
[Queue("Bitcoin", ExchangeName = "EvolvedAI")]
[Serializable]
public class BitcoinSpendMessage
{
public decimal amount { get; set; }
}
[Queue("Bitcoin", ExchangeName = "EvolvedAI")]
[Serializable]
public class BitcoinSpendReceipt
{
public long ID { get; set; }
public decimal amount { get; set; }
public bool success { get; set; }
public DateTime time { get; set; }
}
[Queue("Financial", ExchangeName = "EvolvedAI")]
[Serializable]
public class BondsRequestMessage
{
public DateTime issue { get; set; }
public DateTime maturity { get; set; }
public double coupon { get; set; }
public int frequency { get; set; }
public double yield { get; set; }
public string compounding { get; set; }
public double price { get; set; }
public double calcYield { get; set; }
public double price2 { get; set; }
```

```
public string message { get; set; }
}
[Queue("Financial", ExchangeName = "EvolvedAI")]
[Serializable]
public class BondsResponseMessage
{
public long ID { get; set; }
public DateTime issue { get; set; }
public DateTime maturity { get; set; }
public double coupon {get; set; }
public int frequency { get; set; }
public double yield { get; set; }
public string compounding { get; set; }
public double price { get; set; }
public double calcYield { get; set; }
public double price2 { get; set; }
public string message { get; set; }
}
[Queue("Financial", ExchangeName = "EvolvedAI")]
[Serializable]
public class CreditDefaultSwapRequestMessage
{
public double fixedRate { get; set; }
public double notional { get; set; }
public double recoveryRate {get; set;}
public double fairRate { get; set; }
public double fairNPV { get; set; }
}
[Queue("Financial", ExchangeName = "EvolvedAI")]
[Serializable]
public class CreditDefaultSwapResponseMessage
{
public long ID { get; set; }
public double fixedRate { get; set; }
public double notional { get; set; }
public double recoveryRate { get; set; }
public double fairRate { get; set; }
public double fairNPV { get; set; }
}
[Serializable]
[Queue("Deployments", ExchangeName = "EvolvedAI")]
public class DeploymentStartMessage
{
public long ID { get; set; }
public DateTime Date { get; set; }
}
[Serializable]
[Queue("Deployments", ExchangeName = "EvolvedAI")]
```

```
public class DeploymentStopMessage
{
public long ID { get; set; }
public DateTime Date { get; set; }
}
[Queue("Email", ExchangeName = "EvolvedAI")]
[Serializable]
public class EmailSendRequest
{
public string From;
public string To;
public string Subject;
public string Body;
}
[Serializable]
[Queue("FileSystem", ExchangeName = "EvolvedAI")]
public class FileSystemChangeMessage
{
public long ID { get; set; }
public int ChangeType { get; set; }
public int EventType { get; set; }
public DateTime ChangeDate { get; set; }
public string FullPath { get; set; }
public string OldPath { get; set; }
public string Name { get; set; }
public string OldName { get; set; }
}
[Serializable]
Queue("Health", ExchangeName = "EvolvedAI")]
public class HealthStatusMessage
{
public string ID { get; set; }
public DateTime date { get; set; }
public string serviceName { get; set; }
public int status { get; set; }
public string message { get; set; }
public double memoryUsed { get; set; }
public double CPU { get; set; }
}
[Serializable]
[Queue("Memory", ExchangeName = "EvolvedAI")]
public class MemoryUpdateMessage
{
public long ID { get; set; }
public string Text { get; set; }
public int Gen1CollectionCount { get; set; }
public int Gen2CollectionCount { get; set; }
public float TimeSpentPercent { get; set; }
```

```
public string MemoryBeforeCollection { get; set; }
public string MemoryAfterCollection { get; set; }
public DateTime Date { get; set; }
}
[Serializable]
[Queue("MachineLearning", ExchangeName = "EvolvedAI")]
public class MLMessage
{
public long ID { get; set; }
public int MessageType { get; set; }
public int LayerType { get; set; }
public double param1 { get; set; }
public double param2 { get; set; }
public double param3 { get; set; }
public double param4 { get; set; }
public double replyVal1 { get; set; }
public double replyVal2 { get; set; }
public string replyMsg1 { get; set; }
public string replyMsg2 { get; set; }
}
[Serializable]
[Queue("Trello", ExchangeName = "EvolvedAI")]
public class TrelloResponseMessage
{
public bool Success { get; set; }
public string Message { get; set; }
}
```

Summary

In this chapter, we defined what a microservice and its architecture means to us. We also had an in-depth discussion regarding what we will see as queues and their different configurations. Without any further ado, let's move on and start talking about some of the pieces of our puzzle. We're going to discuss the fantastic world of open source software and take a look at some of the many tools and frameworks we are highlighting in this book in order to create our ecosystem. This entire book is written, and the software is developed, with the sole purpose of you being able to quickly develop a microservice ecosystem, and there is no better way to do this than to leverage the many great open source contributions made.

2
ReflectInsight – Microservice Logging Redefined

Every developer needs to have a good logging tool. Unfortunately, what I mostly see happening is developers keeping up with the latest and greatest of everything but logging. Run it through Log4Net or NLog into a text file and that's it. No richness at all. Welcome to ReflectInsight.

In this chapter, we will:

- Discuss ReflectInsight and how it provides rich logging capabilities
- Discuss all the options available to configure ReflectInsight

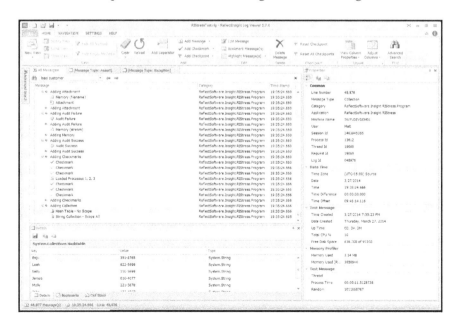

If you have not used ReflectInsight from ReflectSoftware before, you are going to love this chapter. It is so incredibly important to have the right logging tool, especially in machine learning. You absolutely need to know what's going on inside your algorithm, and ReflectSoftware has the richest logging capabilities around. Especially when it comes to machine learning algorithms, there is hands down, nothing that comes close. And when and if you move into deep learning, you are going to be very happy that you can see what is going on. With an algorithm running for possibly days, the insight you receive from the right kind of logging is invaluable.

ReflectInsight is comprised of a **Software Development Kit** (SDK), a router, a Log Viewer, and Live Viewer. We'll take each one separately and discuss them in detail. We'll start with the router.

Router

The router is the central part of the logging system. All log messages are sent to the router, which can distribute the messages from there to listeners such as viewers, text files, binary files, event logs, and databases. You would typically have the router installed on a separate machine from the rest of your logging system, but you do not have to. Once installed and configured (the configuration out of the box is usually suitable for most situations), the router runs as a Windows service and has no user interface:

| > | ⟐ ReflectInsight Router Service | 0% | 9.2 MB | 0 MB/s | 0 Mbps | 0% |

Log Viewer

The Log Viewer is designed to view historical log files that have been saved either manually or from the router/viewer configuration. If you are streaming a high number of messages through the system, you will no doubt collect a lot of log files that may need to be viewed. I wrote an enterprise-grade microservice system for a client that used ReflectInsight at the center of its system, and streamed messages to and through a RabbitMQ system. On average, we streamed roughly one million messages a day (it is still used in production), and, when problems arose, the Log Viewer's historical logging capabilities were invaluable:

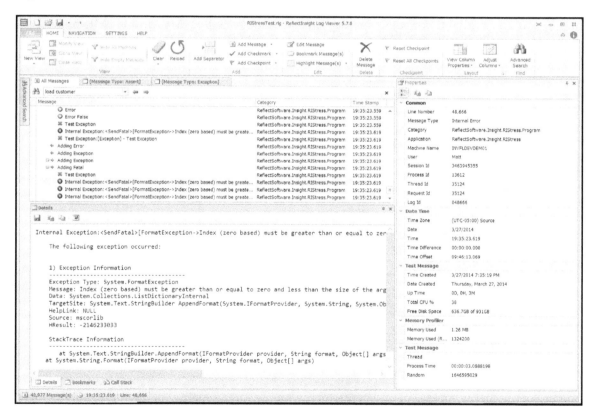

Live Viewer

The Live Viewer is what you will use most of the time to view your real-time logging. The capabilities of the Live Viewer are extensive to say the least. Briefly, the high-performance logging allows us to monitor instrumented applications in real time by displaying log messages in the Live Viewer. We can log incredibly rich details such as Exceptions, Objects, Datasets, Images, Process and Thread Information, and Well-Formatted XML. We can also quickly and easily navigate and trace through our applications to find the information we need. The **Message Details** panel displays the extended details of the selected message. The details could be as simple as the message itself, or complex data such as an object, dataset, binary blob, image, process and thread information, and the content of a collection. Syntax highlighting is available for select message, types such as SQL, XML, and HTML-related messages as well as full Unicode support, which aids in the viewing of these types of messages.

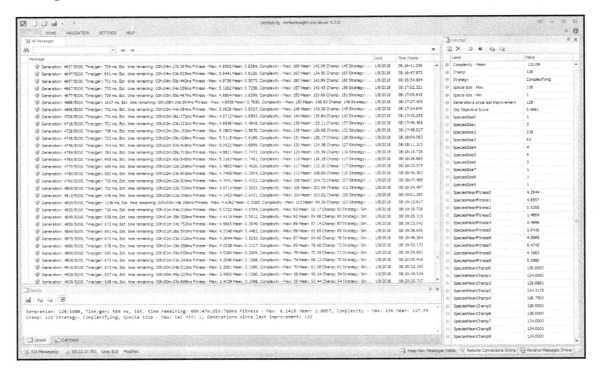

Message navigation

ReflectInsight supports many ways in which to navigate through your logged messages.

You can navigate by using one of the following methods:

- Find a matching **Enter/Exit** method block
- Jump to a parent **Enter/Exit** method block
- Jump from any message in a **User Defined** view to the **All Messages** view
- Go to a message by **Line Number**
- **Advanced Search**
- **Quick Search** (active view only)
- **Message Type** browse navigator
- **Bookmarks**

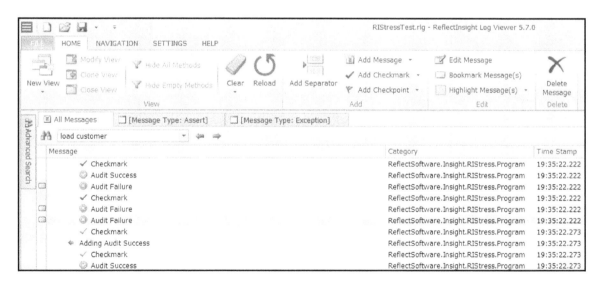

Message properties

This panel allows us to further inspect a selected message. We can view various **Date Time** values, **Time Zone**, **Process Id**, **Thread Id**, **Request Id**, **Category**, **Machine Name**, and so on. We can also extend the message **Properties** panel by attaching user-defined properties to single or multiple messages during our logging:

Watches

Available only in the Live Viewer, the **Watches** panel allows users to display non-persistent information for quick and dirty data change. We can write directly to the **Watches**, or, if using the ReflectInsight **PostSharp AOP** extension, we can easily decorate an object property with a predefined custom attribute. This attribute forces ReflectInsight to display the value of the property whenever its value changes:

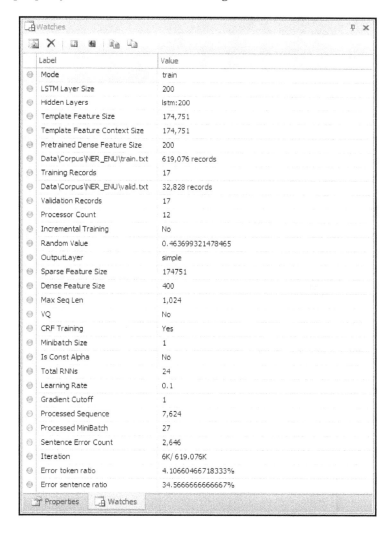

Bookmarks

The **Bookmarks** panel allows us to view bookmarks for the current logging session and it can be persisted with our log file for later retrieval. We can filter bookmarks for the active view, a given view, or see all bookmarks across **All Views**. We can also navigate to any bookmark and immediately activate the view and select where the bookmarked message is located.

Call Stack

The **Call Stack** panel displays the **Call Stack** level of the current selected message. **Call Stack** entries are generated using the **Enter/Exit** methods, or if the message was contained within the `TraceMethod`, using block. We can easily navigate the **Call Stack** by simply double-clicking on a **Call Stack** entry, taking us to the top of the **Enter/Exit** message block within the active message log panel:

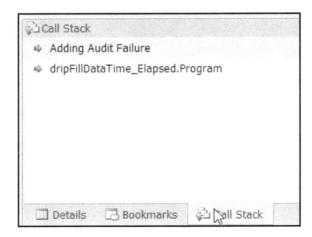

Advanced Search

Here is what the **Advanced Search** dialog looks like. As you can see, you can select the message types as well as many other options that you wish to view:

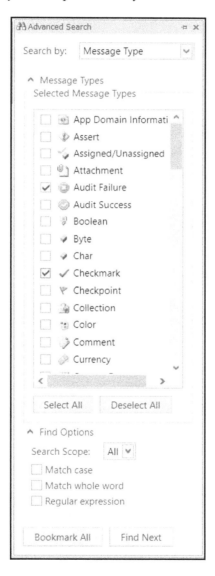

The viewer provides two ways to search messages by criteria.

Quick Search

This is mainly used for simple and quick text-based searching.

Advanced Search

This is primarily used to search messages where a more complex search criterion is needed. Search criteria can include a combination of the following:

- **Message Contents**
- **Message Type**
- **Message Contents AND Type**
- **Message Contents OR Type**
- In addition to **Regular Expression**

The **Advanced Search** view provides the ability to either navigate to the search result or bookmark them.

Time zone formatting

We can display our time details in either **Standard** or **Military** time formats. Select the **Time Zone Type** that best suits your location, such as **Source**, **Local**, **UTC**, or **Custom** by choosing from one of the available system time zones:

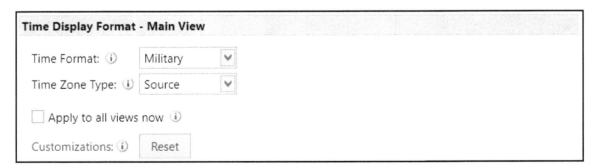

Auto Save/Purge

This is what the **Auto Save/Purge** section looks like:

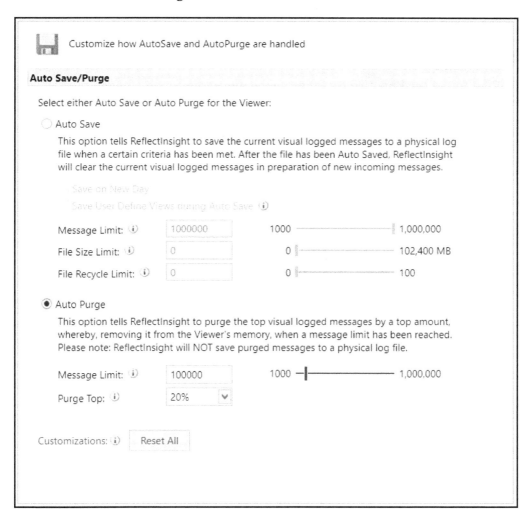

Apart from the library's ability to **Auto Save** rolling log files, the Live Viewer has similar capabilities in addition to **Auto Purge** the top portion of a rolling log file. You can configure the Live Viewer to either **Auto Save** or **Auto Purge** by applying one of the following methods.

Auto Save

This method forces the Live Viewer to save files once a specific criterion has been met (that is on a new day and/or message limit).

Auto Purge

This method forces the Live Viewer to purge the top portion of the logged messages, based on predefined size percentages of the current log file.

Suffice to say that if we look at the following screenshot, we can see that the amount of information able to be gathered from our algorithms and applications is huge:

I've mentioned just how valuable a tool such as this can be when it comes to machine learning, so it's only fair that I show you exactly what I mean. The following is a screenshot of an actual machine learning algorithm outputting data to the Live Viewer. Without this information in real time, we would be lost as to the efficacy and performance of our application!

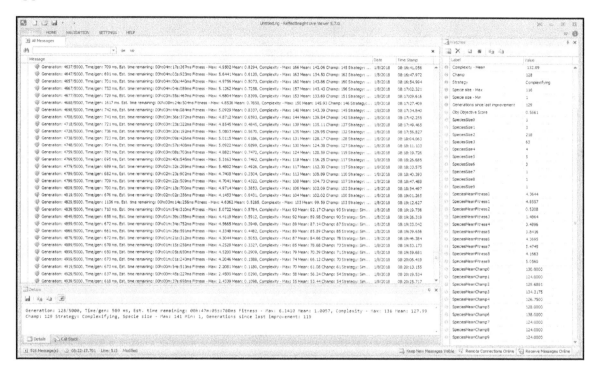

The following screenshot shows the percentages of different messages available in the text we are analyzing:

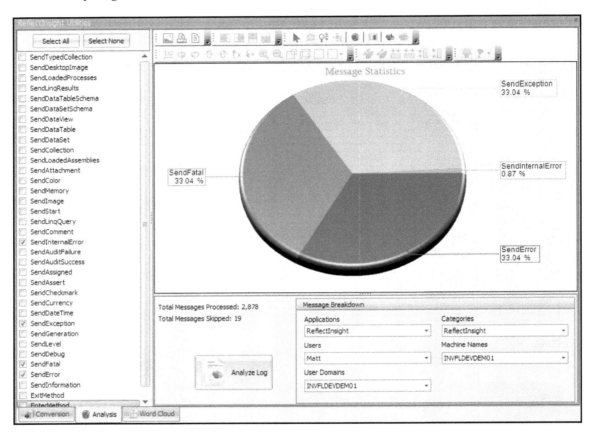

Configuration Editor

In this section, we will cover the things that you need to know about the configuration editor.

Overview

We can use the XML-based configuration file with our applications to make the ReflectInsight viewer behave the way we want it to. There are a few configuration categories, including auto save, filtering, and message coloring.

XML configuration

ReflectInsight is configured using an XML configuration file. The configuration information can be embedded within other XML configuration files such as the application or web .config file, or in a separate file. The configuration is easily readable and updateable, while retaining the flexibility to express all configurations.

Alternatively, ReflectInsight can be configured programmatically. I will use a combination of both throughout this book, with the main configuration usually done via the app.config file.

Dynamic configuration

ReflectInsight automatically monitors its configuration file for changes and dynamically applies these changes when made. In many cases, it is possible to diagnose application issues without terminating the process in question. This can be a very valuable tool in investigating issues from our deployed applications.

Configuration Editor

The **ReflectInsight Configuration Editor** helps in easily creating config files through a visual interface, but advanced users can work with XML.

The tool is very useful for editing settings, defining message patterns/formats, defining extensions, defining listeners, associating colors with message types, and much more.

- Easy-to-understand layout
- Remembers the recent files list
- Pre-defined selections and dynamic section lookups
- Key values pop-up editor

- Message pattern pop-up editor
- Method types pop-up editor
- Color definition and message color pop-up editor

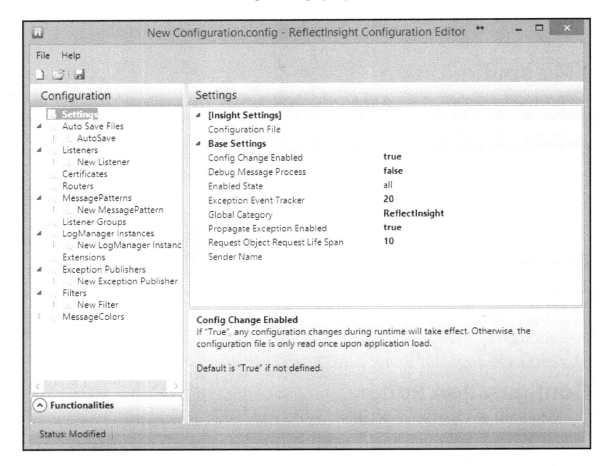

You can download a trial copy of ReflectInsight from www.reflectsoftware.com. Mention this book when purchasing and get a big discount off the retail price!

Summary

In this chapter, we learned about ReflectInsight and the incredible benefits it can provide you with . We saw how it can help a machine learning developer see exactly what is going on inside their algorithm. I encourage you to download your copy and try it out. You will never look at logging the same way again.

Exercises

1. Configure the Live Viewer to meet your specific needs

3
Creating a Base Microservice and Interface

Now the fun begins. We've gotten all the details out of the way, threw a whole bunch of new terms at you, and now we're ready to get to the code. In this chapter, we are going to:

- Create a base microservice that will hold the common functionality that all our microservices can inherit
- This project by all other microservices
- It will supply the interface from which all projects inherit

I will give a note of warning to everyone up front. Even though the purpose (one of the purposes) of a base class is to abstract common details and functionality, for the sake of clarity and understanding in each chapter, I am redundantly showing code that might be included in our base class as it was a part of the microservice itself, and, in some cases, it will be. I would rather provide a basis for you to quickly move forward with your own ecosystem and that means more clarity in the code for the sake of brevity, or just showing how little code we could use. As each microservice is its own entity, sometimes having redundant code in your microservice is a substitute for documentation.

Now, let's talk about base classes for just a moment. Base classes are a useful way to group objects that share a common set of functionalities. Base classes can provide a default set of functionalities, while allowing customization though extensions.

In our case, we will always provide a parameterless constructor for any microservice class. Compilers commonly add a public default constructor to classes that do not define a constructor. This can be misleading to a user of the class, if your intention is for the class not to be creatable. In our case, the **Inversion of Control** (**IoC**) container always requires a parameterless constructor, so we will have it.

Classes versus interfaces

What came first, the chicken or the egg? Should I pass a class or an interface? People will fight over these topics until the cows come home. So why don't we just get knee deep into it and put a stake in the ground. For us, let's define an interface type as a specification of a protocol, potentially supported by many object types. Should we use base classes instead of interfaces whenever possible? From a versioning perspective, classes are more flexible than interfaces. With a class, we can ship version 1.0 and then, in version 2.0, add a new method to the class. As long as the method is not abstract, any existing derived classes continue to function unchanged.

Another potential hazard for us is that because interfaces do not support implementation inheritance, the pattern that applies to classes does not apply to interfaces. Adding a method to an interface is equivalent to adding an abstract method to a base class; any class that implements the interface will break because the class does not implement the new method. In many environments, maintaining backward compatibility is of paramount importance.

Let us say that interfaces are appropriate in the following situations:

- Several unrelated classes want to support a protocol
- These classes already have established base classes (for example, some are user interface controls, and some are XML web services)
- Aggregation is not appropriate or practical

In all other situations, class inheritance is a better model for what we are trying to achieve. Or is it?

If you've been paying intention (pop quiz time), an interface is basically a way of getting around the lack of inheritance in C#, right? What do we mean by lack of inheritance? In a nutshell, in C#, you cannot inherit from multiple classes, but you can inherit from multiple interfaces. Interfaces can also inherit and implement other interfaces as well. Hmmm, this could be the right choice for us.

An interface is a contract, plain and simple. Any implementing class is required to implement everything in the interface. This includes properties, methods, and events. An interface contains only the signatures of the functionality, not the complete concrete implementation. This provides loose coupling, easier maintainability, makes our code more scalable, and makes code reuse much more accessible. The implementation is separate from the interface. This also makes it much easier to create *plug and play* architectures and implement IoC/**Dependency Injection** (**DI**) in your applications.

So what will we do? We will actually implement a mixture of both, inheriting from interfaces when possible and from concrete base classes if the proverbial shoe fits.

Creating our base project

As we mentioned in our previous chapter on Topshelf, all our microservices will be created as console applications. There are, however, two exceptions to this. Both our `Common Messages` project and our `Base MicroService` project will be a **Class Library (.NET Framework)**. They will be referenced by all other projects and will never have the need to run themselves, so we save all that code and overhead.

To start, we should create a new project. Select the project type of **Class Library (.NET Framework)**, label it `Base MicroService`, and click on **OK**, as shown in the following screenshot:

Once done, our base project will be created. We now have an empty base project that looks as follows:

```
namespace Base_MicroService
{
public class Class1
{
}
}
```

Now, let's install our NuGet packages that we will use. First up is an open source package called `CacheManager`. This will provide us with a mechanism for cache management for anyone that requires it. You will see later that our microservice manager also has this package installed and makes good use of it. It's your choice whether or not you want your other microservices to have this capability; we have installed it merely as food for thought, as seen here:

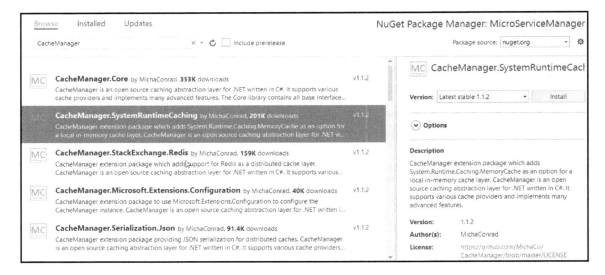

If you have not used `CacheManager` before, I strongly encourage you to read up on it and watch as we implement it throughout our system as our basic caching mechanism. You can learn more about this package at `https://github.com/MichaCo/CacheManager`.

Creating a base interface

As we mentioned previously, an interface is a contract, plain and simple. The interface for our base microservice is going to be relatively simple. The following is what our interface looks like:

```
public interface IBaseMicroService
{
void Start(HostControl hc);
void Stop();
void Pause();
void Continue();
void Shutdown();
void Resume();
void TryRequest(Action action, int maxFailures, int startTimeoutMS = 100,
int resetTimeout = 10000, Action<Exception> OnError = null);
Task TryRequestAsync([NotNull] Func<Task> action, int maxFailures, int
startTimeoutMS = 100, int resetTimeout = 10000, [CanBeNull]
Action<Exception> OnError = null);void PublishMessage(object message,
string connStr = "host=localhost", string topic = "");
Task PublishMessageAsync(object message, string connStr = "host=localhost",
string topic = "");
}
```

You will notice that our interface, aside from the `TryRequest` functions, really only controls the motion of our microservice. This means that every microservice that inherits from this interface must implement these methods. So, let's go ahead and start defining our base microservice and decide what we need to implement. Remember that you can adjust things to your preference as you get up and running.

Creating our base microservice class

Let's start by discussing the member variables that we are going to keep track of. Here they are:

Variables

Here are our variables:

```
/// <summary> The timer. </summary>
private static Timer _timer = null;
```

```
/// <summary> The log. </summary>
readonly static ILog _log =
LogManager.GetLogger(typeof(BaseMicroService<T>));
/// <summary> Identifier for the worker. </summary>
private string _workerId;
/// <summary> The lifetimescope. </summary>
readonly ILifetimeScope _lifetimescope;
/// <summary> The name. </summary>
private static string _name;
/// <summary> The host. </summary>
private static HostControl _host;
/// <summary> The type. </summary>
private static T _type;
/// <summary> The connection factory. </summary>
/// <summary> The bus. </summary>
private IBus _bus;
private ICacheManager<object> _cache = null;
```

The first variable up to bat is our timer. The timer is going to be scheduled to go off every 60 seconds, and with each trigger of the timer, we will send out a Heartbeat message. When we receive this message, our base microservice class will be responsible for packaging that information into our HealthStatus message and publishing it. From there, I am sure you can imagine storing this information in a database, separated by microservice ID, for historical tracking, emailing status results, and many more purposes. Regardless of what we do with it, health monitoring is a very important component of a properly designed microservice ecosystem.

Second, we have our log4net log manager, which will handle logging information for us. We will not cover log4net in this book. There are certainly many good technical references that you can find with a quick internet search.

Third, we have our worker ID. This is Guid represented by a string, which is assigned by the constructor and will serve as the unique identifier for this microservice. Since we will be having many microservices, and since there is nothing stopping multiple instances of the same microservice from running, this unique ID becomes important. This variable will become important once we get to our Bitcoin and microservice manager microservices, since they have the capability for consensus management, and the unique worker ID will be a great help there. But more on that later.

Fourth, we have our lifetime scope variable from our **Autofac** container. The lifetime of something within a microservice is no different than anything else. It is the time that your object lives, from the time you call new until it is disposed. The scope, on the other hand, is the area within the microservice where the object lives, where it can be shared with and among other objects, and so on.

So then, a *lifetime scope* is a combination of both of these. A lifetime scope equates to what some folks call a *unit of work* in an application. The work begins a lifetime scope, services or objects will get resolved from that lifetime scope, and, at the end of that unit of work, you will dispose of the lifetime scope and Autofac will dispose of the resolved services for you automatically. Did you get all of that?

Fifth, we have the name of our microservice. Even though this is an optional parameter, through Topshelf, we will create a practice of always providing it. In addition to providing the name of each microservice, we also concatenate the environmental machine name to the name provided. For example, if your name is ABC and you are running on a machine entitled SomeLaptop, then the name for the microservice will be ABC_SomeLaptop.

Sixth, we have the HostControl. This is a Topshelf component that is passed to our start method and it will be retained to use for stopping the service.

Seventh, we have the type of object our base microservice will be. As a generic class, our BaseMicroService can take many types of classes as its parameter. This means that we will now need to change the signature of our class to this in order to handle generics:

```
public class BaseMicroService<T> where T : class, new()
```

Next, we have the IBus object of EasyNetQ. EasyNetQ's main job in life is to make RabbitMQ easier to work with, which is why this object abstracts away communications, network topology, and more.

And finally, we have the CacheManager object. This CacheManager will be responsible for allowing objects to be stored within an in-memory runtime cache.

Base microservice constructor

We now need to create our BaseMicroService constructor. Inside our constructor, we will create and configure our Heartbeat timer to trigger every 60 seconds, and our worker ID:

```
public BaseMicroService()
{
double interval = 60000;
```

```
_timer = new Timer(interval);
Assumes.True(_timer != null, "_timer is null");
_timer.Elapsed += OnTick;
_timer.AutoReset = true;
_workerId = Guid.NewGuid().ToString();
_name = nameof(T);
}
```

The timer will trigger an event every minute, and that event will be our indication that we need to send our `Heartbeat` message to let everyone know that we are alive and operational. If our service has degraded such, an indication of our circuit breaker pattern coming up, we could send an `Unhealthy` message back saying we are alive but impaired. This `Heartbeat` is aside from what any other microservice may do in regard to health monitoring. Since all microservices will inherit from this base class, the functionality in each method may or may not meet the needs of any one particular situation, so feel free to enhance as required.

I have highlighted the main portion of this code that I want you to pay attention to. I'll be harping about `DateTime` for many chapters to come, so let's just say it again. Consistent timing through the microservice ecosystem is of utmost importance. Notice that the highlighted code is calling the `SystemClock` of Noda Time, and getting us a time relative to our local time zone on the machine we are running from. I use Noda Time religiously, and every major and minor enterprise ecosystem I have built has Noda Time as part of its foundation.

Let's look at our `OnTick` event method:

```
protected virtual void OnTick([NotNull] object sender, [NotNull]
ElapsedEventArgs e)
{
Console.WriteLine(string.Intern("Heartbeat"));
Requires.NotNull<ILog>(_log, string.Intern("log is null"));
_log?.Debug(_name + " (" + _workerId.ToString() + string.Intern("): ") +
SystemClock.Instance.GetCurrentInstant().ToDateTimeUtc().ToLocalTime().ToLo
ngTimeString() + string.Intern(": Heartbeat"));
HealthStatusMessage h = new HealthStatusMessage
{
ID = _workerId,
memoryUsed = Environment.WorkingSet,
CPU = Convert.ToDouble(getCPUCounter()),
date =
SystemClock.Instance.GetCurrentInstant().ToDateTimeUtc().ToLocalTime(),
serviceName = Name,
message = "OK",
status = (int)MSStatus.Healthy
```

```
};
Bus.Publish(h, "HealthStatus");
}
}
```

As you can see, we create a `HealthStatus` message and then publish it for any consumer out there interested in it.

Now, one more time, so we both know we got this. We do not use `DateTime.Now` (highlighted areas) to keep track of our time, we use the `SystemClock` of Noda Time and get the current instant. From there we convert that to a UTC `DateTime`, and then to a local time. As we mentioned, this ensures that every microservice is using the same reference point for the start of time. With the amount of logging we are doing, we really don't want to be relying on the system clocks of individual machines to all be in sync. Once you encounter daylight savings time with an entire ecosystem built and running with Noda Time, you will thank me heavily for this one tip. No more losing messages or doubling them up (more on that in the `Appendix A`, *Best Practices* section at the end of the book).

Implementing our interface

If you remember what we talked about earlier with inheritance, we now need to implement the interface methods we are getting from `IBaseMicroService`. Let's begin with our `Start` method. This method basically configures and starts our timer for us:

```
public virtual bool Start(HostControl hc)
{_host = hc;
Console.WriteLine(_name + string.Intern("Service Started."));
Assumes.True(_timer!= null, string.Intern("_timer is null"));
_timer.AutoReset = true;
_timer.Enabled = true;
_timer.Start();
return true;
}
```

Next comes our `Stop` method. This method will log that our service has stopped, stop our timer, and close our RabbitMQ connections and channels for proper cleanup:

```
public virtual bool Stop()
{
Assumes.True(_log != null, string.Intern("_log is null"));
_log?.Info(_name + string.Intern(" Service is Stopped"));
Assumes.True(_timer != null, string.Intern("_timer is null"));
_timer.AutoReset = false;
```

```
_timer.Enabled = false;
return true;
}
```

The final few methods will remain empty for now aside from logging that they were received. As minor as this may seem, there have been many cases where we suspected a microservice was hung in memory with the process still running. Being able to see that a stop message was given, that power was low, are all invaluable should you ever need to debug any code:

```
public virtual bool Resume()
{
using (var scope = IOCContainer?.BeginLifetimeScope())
{
var logger = scope?.Resolve<MSBaseLogger>();
logger?.LogInformation(Name + " Microservice Resuming");
}
return true;
}
Our Pause method
public virtual bool Pause()
{
using (var scope = IOCContainer?.BeginLifetimeScope())
{
var logger = scope?.Resolve<MSBaseLogger>();
logger?.LogInformation(Name + " Microservice Pausing");
}
return true;
}
Our Continue method
public virtual bool Continue()
{
using (var scope = IOCContainer?.BeginLifetimeScope())
{
var logger = scope?.Resolve<MSBaseLogger>();
logger?.LogInformation(Name + " Microservice Continuing");
}
return true;
}
Our Shutdown method
public virtual bool Shutdown()
{
using (var scope = IOCContainer?.BeginLifetimeScope())
{
var logger = scope?.Resolve<MSBaseLogger>();
logger?.LogInformation(Name + " Microservice Shutting Down");
}
```

```
return true;
}
Last but not least we need to look at our Stop method.
public virtual bool Stop()
{
using (var scope = IOCContainer?.BeginLifetimeScope())
{
var logger = scope?.Resolve<MSBaseLogger>();
logger?.LogInformation(Name + " Microservice Stopping");
}
Assumes.True(_log != null, string.Intern("_log is null"));
_log?.Info(_name + string.Intern(" Service is Stopped"));
Assumes.True(_timer != null, string.Intern("_timer is null"));
_timer.AutoReset = false;
_timer.Enabled = false;
_timer.Stop();
return true;
}
```

This method will be called when our service is stopped. We will log the message and stop our timer.

With all this complete, we now need to implement our `TryRequest` function. These functions will take an action, wrap it in a circuit breaker, and handle any exceptions that might occur. They are basically wrapper functions that we can use to apply the circuit breaker pattern to our microservices, but we don't have to worry about the elegant details:

```
public void TryRequest(Action action, int maxFailures, int startTimeoutMS =
100, int resetTimeout = 10000, Action<Exception> OnError = null)
{
try
{
Requires.True(maxFailures >= 1, "maxFailures must be >= 1");
Requires.True(startTimeoutMS >= 1, "startTimeoutMS must be >= 1");
Requires.True(resetTimeout >= 1, "resetTimeout must be >= 1");
// Initialize the circuit breaker
var circuitBreaker = new CircuitBreaker(
TaskScheduler.Default,
maxFailures: maxFailures,
invocationTimeout: TimeSpan.FromMilliseconds(startTimeoutMS),
circuitResetTimeout: TimeSpan.FromMilliseconds(resetTimeout));
circuitBreaker.Execute(() => action);
}
catch (CircuitBreakerOpenException e1)
{
OnError?.Invoke(e1);
Console.WriteLine(e1.Message);
```

```
}
catch (CircuitBreakerTimeoutException e2)
{
OnError?.Invoke(e2);
Console.WriteLine(e2.Message);
}
catch (Exception e3)
{
OnError?.Invoke(e3);
Console.WriteLine(e3.Message);
}}
```

In this function, we are creating our circuit breaker using the default task scheduler, allowing `maxFailures` failure attempts (usually set to two or three), and specifying when to start and when to reset. After that, we execute the action and handle any exception. In a production application, you would probably want to log any exceptions to a database and send a message to your health monitor application when the circuit breaker opens and closes (more on that later).

Publishing a memory update message

Once we have collected our memory statistics, we will then use this information to publish a memory update message to the system. On the other end, the health monitor microservice could be listening and interested in high watermarks on CPU or memory. Here's what this function looks like:

```
public void PublishMemoryUpdateMessage(int gen1, int gen2, float timeSpent,
string MemoryBefore, string MemoryAfter)
{
// publish a message
MemoryUpdateMessage msg = new MemoryUpdateMessage
{
Text = "Memory MicroService Ran",
Date = SystemClock.Instance.GetCurrentInstant().ToDateTimeUtc(),
Gen1CollectionCount = gen1,
Gen2CollectionCount = gen2,
TimeSpentPercent = timeSpent,
MemoryBeforeCollection = MemoryBefore,
MemoryAfterCollection = MemoryAfter
};
Bus.Publish(msg, "MemoryStatus");
}
Base Logger
```

Our base microservice class also exposes the `ILogger` interface and the `MSBaseLogger` concrete class:

```
public interface ILogger
{
void LogInformation(string message);
void LogWarning(string message);
void LogError(string message);
void LogException(string message, Exception ex);
void LogDebug(string message);
void LogTrace(string message);
}
```

Here's what the concrete class of our `MSBaseLogger` looks like:

```
public class MSBaseLogger : ILogger
{
private void WriteLineInColor(string message, ConsoleColor foregroundColor)
{
Console.ForegroundColor = foregroundColor;
Console.WriteLine(message);
Console.ResetColor();
}
public void LogInformation(string message)
{
RILogManager.Default?.SendInformation(message);
WriteLineInColor(message, ConsoleColor.White);
}
public void LogWarning(string message)
{
RILogManager.Default?.SendWarning(message);
WriteLineInColor(message, ConsoleColor.Yellow);
}
public void LogError(string message)
{
RILogManager.Default?.SendError(message);
WriteLineInColor(message, ConsoleColor.Red);
}
public void LogException(string message, Exception ex)
{
RILogManager.Default?.SendException(message, ex);
WriteLineInColor(message, ConsoleColor.Red);
}
public void LogDebug(string message)
{
RILogManager.Default?.SendDebug(message);
WriteLineInColor(message, ConsoleColor.Blue);
```

```
}
public void LogTrace(string message)
{
RILogManager.Default?.SendTrace(message);
WriteLineInColor(message, ConsoleColor.Cyan);
Trace.WriteLine(message);
}
}
```

Minimal microservice

Before we end this chapter, I want to show you how you can avoid a lot of the code that you see in our `main.cs`. You will still see it throughout the book as it is important for you to understand what is going on and to learn, but abstraction is a big part of what we do. Our minimal Microservice looks as follows:

```
static void Main(string[] args)
{
TopshelfUtility.Run<Microservice>();
}
```

That's it. Some of you may prefer that you use this approach versus the verbose code that you see otherwise. This is a preference that you now have. Only you know your organization best to know what is acceptable and what is not. For your convenience, the advanced filesystem monitor and the base microservice class both have implementations of this in the code for the book, just in case you want to see how it is implemented.

The only other additional thing that you need to do is remove a lot of the code from your microservice and support a new `Start` method as follows:

```
public class Microservice : TopshelfServiceBase
protected override void Process(CancellationToken cancellationToken)
{
}
```

Summary

In this chapter, we designed our base microservice class and interface that we will use for all future microservices. We defined the base functionality that we needed and put that into our base class for others to inherit. I also showed you how to run a very minimalistic microservice as well as where you could locate instances of those running. In the next chapter, we'll look at our common messages and talk about why it's so important that they come from the same namespace.

4
Designing a Memory Management Microservice

This microservice is an example of how you could write your own memory monitoring system for the health of your ecosystem.

In this chapter, we will do the following:

- Start a timer that will trigger every 60 seconds
- Garbage collect our memory and report the status when the timer fires

Of course, we all know there are tons of discussions as to whether the garbage collector of .NET should ever be used, but for the purposes of our example, this will work just fine. Feel free to use whatever tools and tricks you are most comfortable with.

Creating our microservice

The first thing we need to do is create a new project. Remember, we said that all microservices are created as a **Console App (.NET Framework)**. To create this project, we simply select **Add New Project** from the Visual Studio **File** menu and are prompted with the following screen. Next, we select **Console App (.NET Framework)**, as shown in the following screenshot. We will select the **.NET Framework 4.7.1** (used in all microservices), name our microservice `Memory Microservice`, and click **OK**:

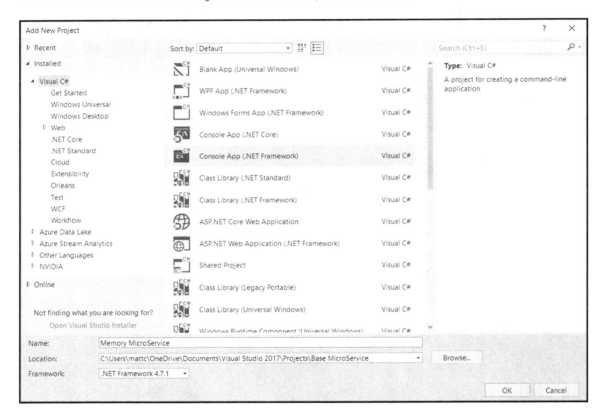

Our code

Now that we have created our project, we need to talk about how we populate our `program.cs` file. This is where our service will be spawned from, and where Topshelf will really show its power. Here's what our fully populated `program.cs` file looks like. I have highlighted some areas that I want you to pay close attention to and understand:

```
static void Main(string[] args)
{
var builder = new ContainerBuilder();
```

Registering our service:

```
builder.RegisterType<MemoryMicroService>()
.AsImplementedInterfaces()
.AsSelf()
?.InstancePerLifetimeScope();
```

Registering our logger:

```
builder.RegisterType<Logger>().SingleInstance();
var container = builder.Build();
```

Watching for `log4net` configuration changes:

```
XmlConfigurator.ConfigureAndWatch(new FileInfo(@".log4net.config"));
HostFactory.Run(c =>
{
```

Using Autofac as our IoC:

```
c?.UseAutofacContainer(container);
c?.UseLog4Net();
c?.ApplyCommandLineWithDebuggerSupport();
c?.EnablePauseAndContinue();
c?.EnableShutdown();
```

Trapping any general exceptions:

```
c?.OnException(ex => { Console.WriteLine(ex.Message); });
c?.Service<MemoryMicroService>(s =>
{
s.ConstructUsingAutofacContainer<MemoryMicroService>();
s?.ConstructUsing(settings =>
{
var service =
AutofacHostBuilderConfigurator.LifetimeScope.Resolve<MemoryMicroService>();
```

```
return service;
});
s?.ConstructUsing(name => new MemoryMicroService());
```

What to do when started, paused, continued, or shut down:

```
s?.WhenStarted((MemoryMicroService server, HostControl host) =>
server.OnStart(host));
s?.WhenPaused(server => server.OnPause());
s?.WhenContinued(server => server.OnResume());
s?.WhenStopped(server => server.OnStop());
s?.WhenShutdown(server => server.OnShutdown());
});
```

Running as a network service:

```
c?.RunAsNetworkService();
```

Starting automatically but giving dependencies a chance to load first:

```
c?.StartAutomaticallyDelayed();
c?.SetDescription(string.Intern("Memory Microservice Sample"));
c?.SetDisplayName(string.Intern("MemoryMicroservice"));
c?.SetServiceName(string.Intern("MemoryMicroService"));
```

If installed as a service, how to handle errors:

```
c?.EnableServiceRecovery(r =>
{
r?.OnCrashOnly();
r?.RestartService(1); //first
r?.RestartService(1); //second
r?.RestartService(1); //subsequents
r?.SetResetPeriod(0);
});
});
```

We'll take each section one by one and describe what's going on.

The first thing we are going to do is create our Autofac container by creating a `builder` object and registering our `MemoryMicroService` and `Logger` classes. Once we are done registering all of our types and interfaces, we can build our container:

```
var builder = new ContainerBuilder();
// Service itself
builder.RegisterType<MemoryMicroService>()
.AsImplementedInterfaces()
.AsSelf()
```

```
?.InstancePerLifetimeScope();
builder.RegisterType<Logger>().SingleInstance();
var container = builder.Build();
```

Next, we tell our XmlConfigurator object of log4net to use the log4net configuration file for configuration, and to listen for changes. Listening for changes will also update the configuration objects if changed:

```
XmlConfigurator.ConfigureAndWatch(new FileInfo(@".log4net.config"));
```

Now comes the fun part. The majority of our code is going to sit inside our HostFactory class, which has the Run method. Let's start by taking it one step at a time and breaking it down:

```
HostFactory.Run(c =>
{
c?.UseAutofacContainer(container);
c?.UseLog4Net();
c?.ApplyCommandLineWithDebuggerSupport();
c?.EnablePauseAndContinue();
c?.EnableShutdown();
c?.OnException(ex => { Console.WriteLine(ex.Message); });
```

This first part tells the program that, instead of the internal IoC container of Topshelf, we are using the Autofac container instead. Next, we will use log4net as our logger. Then, our next command applies command-line parameter support with a debugger. Next, we enable pause and continue, as well as shutdown commands, allowing our microservice to respond to and process these Windows service commands. Finally, we handle any exceptions by writing them to the console. In a production environment, you might want to log exceptions to a database.

Here's the following section:

```
s?.ConstructUsing(name => new MemoryMicroService());
s?.WhenStarted((MemoryMicroService server, HostControl host) =>
server.OnStart(host));
s?.WhenPaused(server => server.OnPause());
s?.WhenContinued(server => server.OnResume());
s?.WhenStopped(server => server.OnStop());
s?.WhenShutdown(server => server.OnShutdown());
```

First, we tell Topshelf we are using our constructor to create our microservice. The next five commands tell Topshelf what to do with each of the start, stop, pause, continue, and shutdown commands. For us, they call a similarly named command inside our microservice object. Remember that the base class implements the basic logic, so if all we want is to just log that the command is received and do nothing else, then just call the base object.

The following command will allow the microservice to run as a network service. Feel free to quickly change this to whatever policies your organization adheres to as far as running Windows services:

```
c?.RunAsNetworkService();
```

This equates to the service **Log On** properties stored for each service. Services can run as a network or **Local System account**:

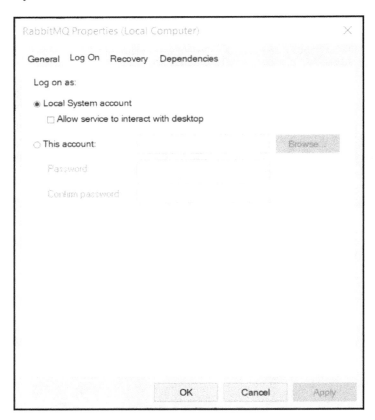

By the way, do you remember which account does what? In case you don't have it memorized, here are the basic guidelines:

- **Local System account** is a very high-privileged built-in account. It has extensive privileges on the local system and acts as the computer on the network. The actual name of the account is `NT AUTHORITYSYSTEM`.
- The **Local Service account** is a built-in account that has the same level of access to resources and objects as members of the users group. This limited access helps safeguard the system if individual services or processes are compromised. Services that run as the **Local Service account** access network resources as a null session without credentials. The actual name of the account is `NT AUTHORITYLOCAL SERVICE`.
- The **Network Service account** is a built-in account that has more access to resources and objects than members of the users group. Services that run as the **Network Service account** access network resources by using the credentials of the computer account. The actual name of the account is `NT AUTHORITYNETWORK SERVICE`.

The following command will allow the microservice to start automatically, but delayed, in case dependent services need to start first:

```
c?.StartAutomaticallyDelayed();
```

Next, we have to tell Topshelf the service name, display name, and description of our microservice. The service name is optional and, by default, uses the namespace of `program.cs` (the calling assembly type namespace). The service name should never contain spaces or other whitespace characters. Each service on our system must have a unique name. Also, the description and display names are optional and default to the service name:

```
c?.SetDescription(string.Intern("Memory Microservice Sample"));
c?.SetDisplayName(string.Intern("MemoryMicroservice"));
c?.SetServiceName(string.Intern("MemoryMicroService"));
```

Finally, we inform Topshelf how we want our microservice to handle recoveries in the event of a fatal execution sequence. In this case, we are only going to restart on a crash, and restart on the first, second, and subsequent attempts:

```
c?.EnableServiceRecovery(r =>
{
r?.OnCrashOnly();
r?.RestartService(1); //first
r?.RestartService(1); //second
```

```
r?.RestartService(1); //subsequents
r?.SetResetPeriod(0);
});
```

These fields map to the fields in the service control manager (service properties), as you can see in the following screenshot:

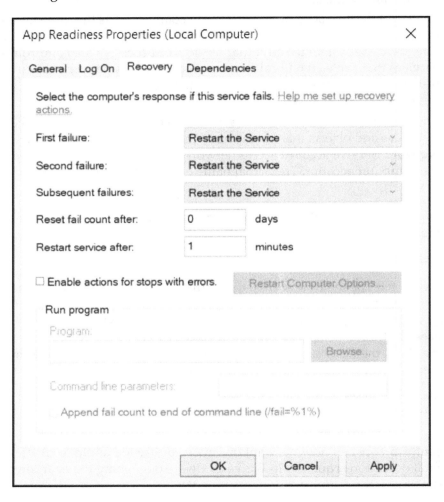

Reclaiming memory

Since our microservice is about memory, let's create a simple routine to invoke the garbage collector, reclaim memory, and then report the results back to us. We will start by using our `Start` method to create a timer that will trigger every 60 seconds:

```
public bool Start([CanBeNull] HostControl host)
{
base.Start(host);
hc = host;
const double interval = 60000;
_timer = new Timer(interval);
_timer.Elapsed += OnTick;
Console.WriteLine(string.Intern("MemoryMicroService Started."));
return (true);
}
```

The method that our timer calls is the `OnTick` method. Each time this triggers, we will, in turn, call our `ReclaimMemory` function, which will invoke the garbage collector and reclaim memory. After it has completed this, it will report back memory both before and after collection, as well as the garbage collection count for each generation:

```
protected virtual void OnTick(object sender, ElapsedEventArgs e)
{
Console.WriteLine(string.Intern("Reclaiming Memory"));
ReclaimMemory();
}
/// <summary> Reclaim memory. </summary>
public static void ReclaimMemory()
{
```

Log the memory before the operation:

```
long mem2 = GC.GetTotalMemory(false);
Console.WriteLine(string.Intern("*** Memory ***"));
Console.WriteLine(string.Intern("tMemory before GC: ") + ToBytes(mem2));
```

Handle the large object heap compaction:

```
GCSettings.LargeObjectHeapCompactionMode =
GCLargeObjectHeapCompactionMode.CompactOnce;
GC.Collect();
GC.WaitForPendingFinalizers();
```

Record the memory again:

```
long mem3 = GC.GetTotalMemory(false);
Console.WriteLine(string.Intern("tMemory after GC: ") + ToBytes(mem3));
Console.WriteLine("tApp memory being used: " +
ToBytes(Environment.WorkingSet));
int gen1=0;
int gen2=0;
for (int x = 0; x < GC.MaxGeneration; x++)
{
if (x == 0)
gen1 = GC.CollectionCount(x);
else if (x == 1)
gen2 = GC.CollectionCount(x);
Console.WriteLine("ttGeneration " + (x) + " Collection Count: " +
GC.CollectionCount(x));
}
const string category = ".NET CLR Memory";
const string counter = "% Time in GC";
string instance = Process.GetCurrentProcess().ProcessName;
float percent= 0.0F;
if (PerformanceCounterCategory.Exists(category) &&
PerformanceCounterCategory.CounterExists(counter, category) &&
PerformanceCounterCategory.InstanceExists(instance, category))
{
var gcPerf = new PerformanceCounter(category, counter, instance);
percent = gcPerf.NextValue();
string suffix = "%";
if (percent > 50.0)
{
suffix += " <- High Watermark Warning";
}
Console.WriteLine("ttTime Spent in GC: " + $"{percent:00.##}" + suffix);
}
Subscribe();
```

Publish our message:

```
PublishMessage(gen1, gen2, percent, ToBytes(mem2), ToBytes(mem3));
Console.WriteLine(string.Intern("*** Memory ***")); }
}
```

This is what our microservice looks like when it's running. You can see that the base class is sending out Heartbeat every five seconds. We did this, of course, so that we did not have to repeat the same code over and over again for each microservice. You can also see that the microservice reclaims memory and prints out exactly what it is doing every 60 seconds:

Dynamically creating an exchange

Now that our microservice is reclaiming our memory as we intended, we need to stop and make sure that we have a basic understanding of how our communication mechanism between microservices is going to work. In order to connect and publish our message, we needed to dynamically ensure that both our exchange and queue have been created. We do this in our `Subscribe` method, as shown in the following code snippet:

```
public static void Subscribe()
{
Bus = RabbitHutch.CreateBus("host=localhost",
x => x.Register<IConventions, AttributeBasedConventions>());
```

Declare the `exchange`:

```
IExchange exchange = Bus.Advanced.ExchangeDeclare("EvolvedAI",
ExchangeType.Topic);
```

Declare the `queue`:

```
IQueue queue = Bus.Advanced.QueueDeclare("Memory");
```

Bind the queue to the exchange for message delivery using the Bind function:

```
Bus.Advanced.Bind(exchange, queue, "");
}
```

With the previous code executed step by step, you can see that the exchange has now been created:

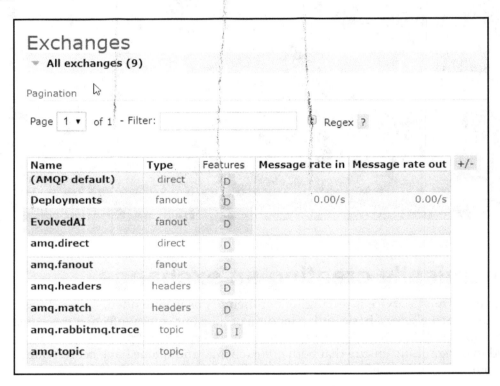

At this point, there is still no queue associated with the exchange for messages to flow through.

Dynamically creating a queue

Once we have our exchange created, we have to create a queue that can be bound to it. Queues have names so that they can be easily referenced. We can choose to provide our own queue names (which we will) or pass an empty string and have the name be generated automatically for us.

Queues have properties that we can pass to them, or use the defaults for. The properties are as follows:

- Queue name
- A durable queue will survive a service restart
- Exclusive will be used by only one connection and the queue will be deleted when that connection closes
- Auto-delete any queue that has had at least one consumer when the last consumer unsubscribes
- Arguments are optional and are server-specific name value pairs

You can think of queues as ordered collections of messages, which are consumed in **First In First Out (FIFO)** order. There is an exception for priority and sharded queues, but that is beyond the scope of this book.

What happens if we declare a queue as durable? Well, durable queues are persisted to disk and therefore survive microservice restarts. Non-durable queues are also called **transient**. It is your choice as to what you prefer to use; I prefer to keep the queues durable myself and that is the convention we will stick to in this book.

Let me point out though that just because a queue is durable does not mean that the messages going to that queue are also durable. If the service is restarted, the durable queue will be recreated during startup, but only messages marked as 'persistent' will also be recovered.

Another note about queues that we should mention is that a queue keeps messages in RAM and/or on disk, depending if they are declared persistent. Publishing a transient message will result in that message remaining in RAM when possible. It should be noted that if a queue comes under memory pressure, it will page these messages out to disk.

Since we mentioned it, let's talk a little bit about memory pressure so you can better understand how RabbitMQ handles this. The RabbitMQ server detects the total amount of RAM installed on the computer it is running on. By default (which we will not change), once the server uses above 40% of this memory (sometimes referred to as the 'memory high watermark'), it will raise a memory alarm and clock all connections that are publishing messages. Normal service resumes once the memory condition is cleared.

Keep in mind that 32 bit architectures have a memory limit of 2 GB. Most 64 bit architectures under Windows have an 8 TB limit (although AMD and Intel EM64T raise this to 256 TB). Also note that even under a 64 bit operating system, a 23 bit process only has a maximum address space of 2 GB.

With all that out of the way, let's take a look at our `Subscribe` method and see how we create our `queue` and `Bind` it to `exchange`:

```
public static void Subscribe()
{
Bus = RabbitHutch.CreateBus("host=localhost",
x => x.Register<IConventions, AttributeBasedConventions>());
IExchange exchange = Bus.Advanced.ExchangeDeclare("EvolvedAI",
ExchangeType.Topic);
IQueue queue = Bus.Advanced.QueueDeclare("Memory");
Bus.Advanced.Bind(exchange, queue, "");
}
```

When the exchange is created and the queue is bound, the RabbitMQ Control Panel will show the following information. As you can see, the `Memory` queue is bound to this exchange (`EvolvedAI`); the exchange is a **fanout** exchange, and is durable, meaning it will survive restarts:

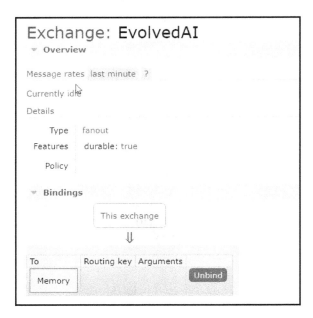

Publishing a message

When we publish a message, there are various utilities that the RabbitMQ Control Panel provides to view exchanges, queues, and message traffic.

The following is a snapshot of our exchange immediately after a message is published:

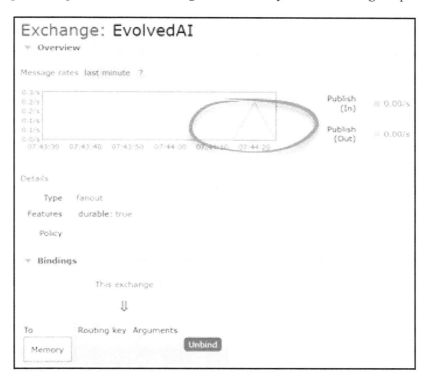

And here is a screenshot after several deployment messages have been sent:

Overview			Messages			Message rates		
Name	Features	**State**	**Ready**	**Unacked**	**Total**	**incoming**	**deliver / get**	**ack**
Deployments	D	idle	5	0	5	0.00/s		
HealthMonitor	D	idle	0	0	0			
JobScheduler	D	idle	0	0	0			
Memory	D	idle	0	0	0			

The next thing that I want to do is to walk you through what you will see in the RabbitMQ Control Panel, as the visuals make everything self-explanatory. The following is a screenshot showing that a consumer was connected to our exchange and received a message. This is denoted by the **Publish (Out)** message rate indicated in blue (for those viewing this book in black and white, this will be the triangular line shown at the **07:44:20** minute marker):

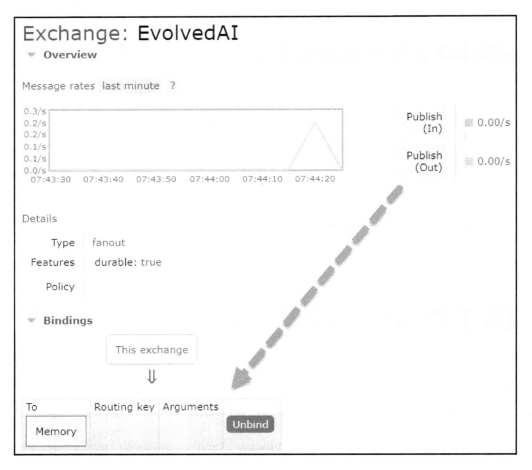

The following screenshot shows our message queue (**Memory**) after three deployment messages have been published by our microservice. We have no consumers on the other end to consume the message, so the messages, as we indicated earlier, remain in the queue until a consumer connects and subscribes to a topic that matches our message:

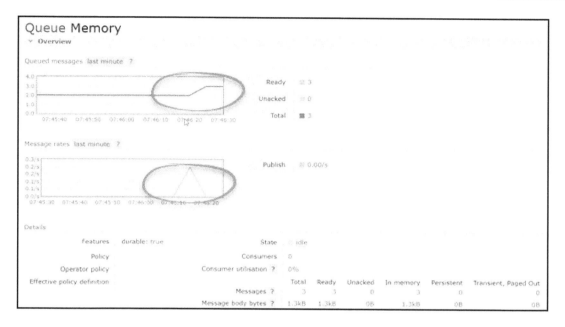

Here is a screenshot of our queue with three memory status messages sent. Additionally, you can see the output from the program alongside it. You can see that, over the **last minute**, we have held steady in the number of messages published to this **Exchanges** and **Queues**:

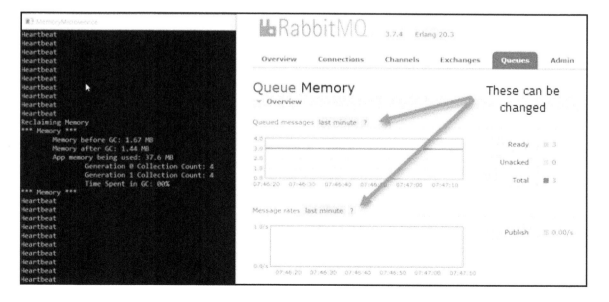

Summary

In this chapter, we created our memory management microservice. We talked about how to create exchanges and queues, as well as how we connect to both. We also published several messages and saw the effects reflected within the RabbitMQ Control Panel. You've created a microservice, gathered memory statuses, and published several messages. Congratulations!

In the next chapter, we'll focus on what happens during your microservice deployment and see how we can use our microservice framework to assist with that.

Exercises

1. In the RabbitMQ Control Panel, create a new username and password instead of using the default guest/guest
2. Log errors and exceptions to a database for later retrieval

5
Designing a Deployment Monitor Microservice

During a deployment, whether it is for your microservices or something else, you are inevitably going to have to start and stop services and applications as a part of your deployment process. I am assuming here you have a managed, continuous deployment process, or, at the very least, not a manual process (yes, I've seen big clients manually promote across environment by hand picking change sets!).

In this chapter we will learn:

- How to create a deployment monitor microservice
- How to create messages specifically for this microservice
- How to handle events during a deployment
- How to tell if a deployment has taken too much time

Now, let's talk a little about what a typical deployment scenario might look like:

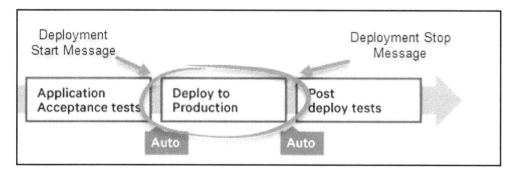

When a deployment starts, one or more services and applications affected in that environment (QA, staging, production, and so on) will have to be stopped to be updated. When this happens, the system is basically inoperable for the time period of the deployment.

Let me ask you this. How many folks can remember a deployment process that failed for one reason or another, and the next morning you came in to work only to find nothing working? By developing a deployment monitor microservice, we are attempting to mitigate this and other problem scenarios we might encounter. First and foremost, we are going to stop monitoring health checks for our system because there won't be any status being reported! The last thing we want to do is to start sending health alerts for our microservices not responding when the lack of response is known and valid.

Sending alerts and messages is a very important part of what this ecosystem does, and a huge value add to tell upper management. But be careful to avoid being the boy who always cried wolf. One day, the wolf will be there, and no one will be listening! I would advise sending messages to yourself until everything is perfected. While you are testing and perfecting the microservice, you should not send any email messages outside your own development arena. Even though I always tried to believe that transparency will be very beneficial, everyone wants transparency until everything becomes transparent! So don't send alert messages outside your close knit group until you are fully ready to explain what the root cause is and what the corrective action is. Otherwise, it's just another non-intuitive error message upper management is seeing and not understanding.

In talking about deployment processes that fail, we all know that there are times where a deployment fails or hangs for various reasons. The more your continuous development process becomes automated, the more likely it is you will encounter a deployment that did not complete correctly, for a plethora of reasons. In the microservice world, this is even more so than with applications, as our microservices support starting and stopping. What do we do if we are asked to stop when we are in the middle of processing messages? This and other questions need to be answered for us to be able to implement the microservice correctly. So, a good practice is that when the deployment monitoring microservice receives a message that a deployment has started, start a timer for a specific interval, say, 15 minutes. As soon as we receive the `DeploymentStopMessage`, stop the timer. If the 15 minutes elapses and we haven't yet received our `DeploymentStopMessage`, then we know there is a problem and we can begin to handle it, and hopefully mitigate the problem as well. Ultimately, we will need to send an alert email to notify users that the deployment is experiencing problems. I would recommend waiting until you gather as much information as you can so that your alert message is complete, intuitive, and is seen as valuable by all.

Deployment issues

We are now going to talk a bit about why deployments fail. Of course, the reasons could be countless, it seems like there's always something popping up somewhere, and the first thing an end user tests is probably the one thing we did not expect. But let's assume for a moment that we did everything right. What kind of problems do we face when it comes to deployments?

The first category of deployment issues is essentially about correctness from a software perspective. Our microservice might make all sorts of demands about the environment in which it executes; that certain other components are present in the system, that certain configuration files exist, that certain modifications were made to the Windows registry, and so on. If any of those environmental characteristics does not hold, then there is a possibility that the software does not work the same as it did on our development machine. Some concrete issues are:

- Even though a microservice should be self-contained, this is not always the case; rather, it depends on other components to do some work on its behalf. These are its dependencies. For a correct deployment, it is necessary that all dependencies are identified. This identification is quite hard, however, as it is often difficult to test whether the dependency specification is complete. After all, if we forget to specify a dependency, we don't discover that fact if the machine on which we are testing already happens to have the dependency installed.
- Dependencies also need to be compatible with what is expected by the referring component. In general, not all versions of a component will work. This is the case even in the presence of type-checked interfaces, since interfaces never give a full specification of the observable behavior of a component.

Also, components often exhibit build-time variability, meaning that they can be built with or without certain optional features, or with other parameters selected at build time. Even worse, the component might be dependent on a specific compiler, or on specific compilation options being used for its dependencies:

- Components can depend on non-software artifacts, such as configuration files, and user accounts.
- Components can require certain hardware characteristics, such as a specific processor type or a video card. These are somewhat outside the scope of software deployment, since we can at most check for such properties, not realize them if they are missing.

- Finally, deployment can be a distributed problem. A component can depend on other components running on remote machines or as separate processes on the same machine. For instance, a typical multi-tier web service consists of an HTTP server, a server implementing the business logic, and a database server, possibly all running on different machines.

So, we have two problems in deployment; we must identify what our component's requirements on the environment are, and we must somehow realize those requirements in the target environment. Realization might consist of installing dependencies, creating or modifying configuration files, starting remote processes, and so on. As you can see, it's many times easier to say than it is to do!

Installation

For this project, we will create another console application and name it `DeploymentMonitorMicroService`. We will follow the same process as we have with other microservices so that you become 100% familiar with it:

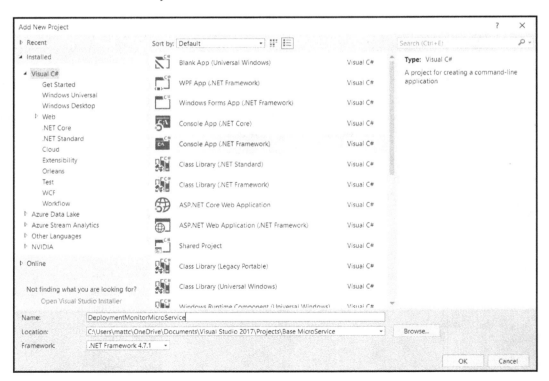

Our messages

For this microservice, we will have both a deployment `Start` and `Stop` method. This will provide us with the capability to signal all willing recipients that a deployment has started and stopped.

Deployment start message

Here is what the `DeploymentStartMessage` looks like:

```
/// <summary> A deployment start message. </summary>
[Serializable]
[Queue("Deployments", ExchangeName = "EvolvedAI")]
public class DeploymentStartMessage
{
 public long ID { get; set; }
 public DateTime Date { get; set; }
}
```

Deployment stop message

And here is what our `DeploymentStopMessage` looks like:

```
/// <summary> A deployment stop message. </summary>
[Serializable]
[Queue("Deployments", ExchangeName = "EvolvedAI")]
public class DeploymentStopMessage
{
 public long ID { get; set; }
 public DateTime Date { get; set; }
}
```

Our program

Once we have populated our main program file, it will look as follows. Notice that it mirrors that of all the other microservices we have created. Why continue to show the same code? Because this really is the heart of how each microservice operates, and it's so very important for you to gain an understanding of this. Even if most of the code is identical, as you become more familiar with it, you will be in a much better position to make the changes needed for your environment. And pay attention, because pretty soon we're going to start changing it up a bit to show you even more things you can do and accomplish:

```
static void Main(string[] args)
{
var builder = new ContainerBuilder();
// Service itself
builder.RegisterType<Logger>().SingleInstance();
builder.RegisterType<DeploymentMonitorMicroservice>()
.AsImplementedInterfaces()
.AsSelf()
?.InstancePerLifetimeScope();
var container = builder.Build();
XmlConfigurator.ConfigureAndWatch(new
FileInfo(@".log4net.config"));
HostFactory.Run(c =>
{
 c?.UseAutofacContainer(container);
 c?.UseLog4Net();
 c?.ApplyCommandLineWithDebuggerSupport();
 c?.EnablePauseAndContinue();
 c?.EnableShutdown();
 c?.OnException(ex => { Console.WriteLine(ex.Message); });
 c?.Service<DeploymentMonitorMicroservice>(s =>
 {
   s.ConstructUsingAutofacContainer
     <DeploymentMonitorMicroservice>   ();
   s?.ConstructUsing(settings =>
 {
var service =  AutofacHostBuilderConfigurator.LifetimeScope.
Resolve<DeploymentMonitorMicroservice>();
 return service;
});
s?.ConstructUsing(name => new DeploymentMonitorMicroservice());
s?.WhenStarted((DeploymentMonitorMicroservice server, HostControl host) =>
server.OnStart(host));
s?.WhenPaused(server => server.OnPause());
s?.WhenContinued(server => server.OnResume());
s?.WhenStopped(server => server.OnStop());
```

```
s?.WhenShutdown(server => server.OnShutdown());
});
c?.RunAsNetworkService();
c?.StartAutomaticallyDelayed();
c?.SetDescription(string.Intern
   ("Deployment Monitor Microservice Sample"));
c?.SetDisplayName(string.Intern("DeploymentMonitorMicroservice"));
c?.SetServiceName(string.Intern("DeploymentMonitorMicroservice"));
c?.EnableServiceRecovery(r =>
{
r?.OnCrashOnly();
r?.RestartService(1); //first
r?.RestartService(1); //second
r?.RestartService(1); //subsequents
r?.SetResetPeriod(0);
});
});
}
```

With that out of the way, let's focus on creating our DeploymentMonitorMicroservice class itself. We'll start by showing our variables:

```
private IBus _bus;
private bool _deploymentInProgress;
private Timer _deploymentTimer;
private Timer _healthTimer;
```

Next, our constructor will set Name of our microservice:

```
public DeploymentMonitorMicroservice()
{
Name = "Deployment Monitor Microservice";
}
```

Our OnStart method will call the base Start method, create both our deployment and health timers, and then create our exchange and queue:

```
public new bool OnStart([CanBeNull] HostControl hc)
{
base.Start(hc);
if (_bus == null)
_bus = RabbitHutch.CreateBus("host=localhost");
_deploymentInProgress = false;
if (_deploymentTimer == null)
_deploymentTimer = new Timer();
_deploymentTimer.Interval = 6000 * 15; // give it 15 minutes
_deploymentTimer.Enabled = true;
```

```
_deploymentTimer.Elapsed += _deploymentTimer_Elapsed;
_deploymentTimer.AutoReset = true;
_deploymentTimer.Start();
if(_healthTimer == null)
_healthTimer = new Timer();
_healthTimer.Interval = 60000;
_healthTimer.Enabled = true;
_healthTimer.AutoReset = true;
_healthTimer.Elapsed += _healthTimer_Elapsed;
_healthTimer.Start();
CreateTopology("EvolvedAI", "Management", "");
return (true);
}
```

Subscribing to messages

Here is our code for subscribing to our deployment messages. As in previous chapters, we create our connection to RabbitMQ, create our `exchange` and `queue`, bind them together, and then subscribe to our messages, providing the procedure we will use to process our messages:

```
public void Subscribe()
{
Bus = RabbitHutch.CreateBus("host=localhost",
x =>
{
x.Register<IConventions, AttributeBasedConventions>();
x.EnableMessageVersioning();
});
IExchange exchange = Bus.Advanced.ExchangeDeclare
  ("EvolvedAI", ExchangeType.Topic);\
IQueue queue = Bus.Advanced.QueueDeclare("Deployments");
Bus.Advanced.Bind(exchange, queue, "");
Bus.Subscribe<DeploymentStartMessage>("Deployment.Start", msg => {
ProcessDeploymentStartMessage(msg); },
config => config.WithTopic("Deployments"));
Bus.Subscribe<DeploymentStopMessage>("Deployment.Stop", msg => {
ProcessDeploymentStopMessage(msg); },
config => config.WithTopic("Deployments"));
}
```

Processing messages

After configuring our `queue` and `exchange`, we then subscribe to both the deployment start and stop messages. When our deployment start message arrives, we kick off our timer. If the deployment stop message arrives prior to our time limit, we will stop the timer without incident. If the deployment stop message does not arrive prior to our time limit, we will alert the user:

```
public void ProcessDeploymentStartMessage
(DeploymentStartMessage msg)
{
__deploymentTimer.Stop();
__deploymentTimer.Start();
}
public void ProcessDeploymentStopMessage(DeploymentStopMessage msg)
{
__deploymentTimer.Stop();
}
```

Publishing health status messages

When our health timer elapses, our `_healthTimer_Elapsed` method will be called. When this happens, we will create our `HealthStatusMessage` with all the information populated, and then publish the message. Remember, no `DateTime`. Now, anywhere within our codebase:

```
private void _healthTimer_Elapsed(object sender,
ElapsedEventArgs e)
{
HealthStatusMessage h = new HealthStatusMessage
{
ID = ID,
memoryUsed = Environment.WorkingSet,
CPU = Convert.ToDouble(getCPUCounter()),
date =
SystemClock.Instance.GetCurrentInstant().ToDateTimeUtc().ToLocalTime(),
serviceName = "Deployment Monitor MicroService",
message = "OK",
status = (int) MSStatus.Healthy
};
PublishMessage(h, "EvolvedAI", "");
}
```

When we publish this `HealthStatusMessage`, we will include the CPU and memory usage of our program. I have found that it's great to have this information available should you ever have an errant or zombie microservice that has a mind of its own. This will give you a detailed history of how your microservice performed up to a point of failure if one occurs. Just store the information into a SQL or NoSQL database for historical purposes and you are all set. I can't tell you how many times I have seen a microservice not responding and the first indication is that memory usage is unusually high. Plotting a trend line on a chart showing the memory usage, or alternatively a histogram, is also another big value add if it's ever needed. And trust me on this one, it's never needed until something goes wrong!

As soon as the microservice receives its deployment start message, it kicks off a deployment timer, and uses that time to monitor the length of the deployment. In our sample, if that timer expires after 15 minutes without us receiving the deployment stop message, we know that the deployment took too long, and we need to alert the user. I'll leave it as an exercise to the reader to make this parameter passable to the function. You could also pass an action to denote what to do when and if the deployment does take too long. You could send an email, log it into a SQL or NoSQL database, trigger a Syslog or Windows event viewer message, and so much more. This is one area where you get to customize this microservice to best fit your individual needs!

Here is what our deployment timer event looks like:

```
private void _deploymentTimer_Elapsed(object sender, ElapsedEventArgs e)
{
if (_deploymentInProgress)
Console.WriteLine("ERROR: Deployment is taking too long");
}
```

Summary

In this chapter, we discussed deployments and many of the reasons as to why deployments sometimes fail. We created a deployment monitor microservice that is designed to monitor the length of our deployments. We talked about how and why an alert will be triggered if the deployment time exceeds a certain threshold. We also showed several ways in which you could customize this microservice to better fit the needs of you and your organization.

Exercises

1. Complete this microservice such that it fully handles a deployment from start to finish
2. Send an alert email when a deployment is not finished within the allotted time
3. Notify the microservice manager about the status of every deployment

6
Designing a Scheduling Microservice

One of the solutions for which a microservice serves a very useful purpose is that of scheduling jobs. If you follow a true separation of concerns pattern, separating this functionality into its own business unit, that is, a microservice, is the correct thing to do. In this chapter, we are going to create a microservice that does just that. We will also gain exposure to **Quartz.NET**, a fabulous open source job scheduling platform.

The difference with this microservice over others is that it does not accept or respond to messages. Even though that is the heart of our ecosystem, I want to show you that there's no harm in having a mix of microservices doing your work. Not everything needs to have or send a message. This microservice will be your job executor that is performing pre-defined work. Can it send and accept messages? Absolutely. You could send all your job parameters to the microservice and have it execute as required. The possibilities are endless.

In this chapter, we will:

- Develop a scheduling microservice
- Show you how to use Quartz.NET to perform all your job scheduling

Let's get on with showing you how to execute jobs.

Installation

For this microservice, we will create a **Console App (.NET Framework)** just like we have for all the other microservices:

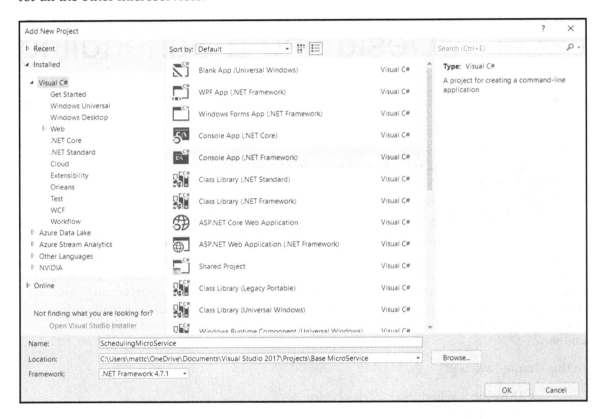

Installing Quartz.NET

To install Quartz.NET, we are going to install the NuGet package of the same name, as shown in the following screenshot. Please take the latest stable version if you are installing it yourself in one of your own projects:

What is Quartz.NET?

So what exactly is this Quartz.NET you might be asking? Without a doubt, it is one of, if not the premier, job scheduler framework around. It is full-featured, it is open source, and it can scale from the smallest of jobs up to large scale enterprise systems.

So why should we choose Quartz? Let's show you some of the benefits of using Quartz and we'll let you decide.

Runtime environments

The following are the environments in which Quartz.NET can be used:

- Quartz.NET can run embedded within another free-standing application or microservice (as we are doing here)
- Quartz.NET can run as a standalone program (within its own .NET virtual machine instance), to be used via **.NET Remoting**
- Quartz.NET can be instantiated as a cluster of standalone programs (with load balance and failover capabilities)

Job scheduling

Jobs are scheduled to run when a given trigger occurs. Triggers can be created with nearly any combination of the following directives:

- At a certain time of day (to the millisecond)
- On certain days of the week
- On certain days of the month
- On certain days of the year
- Not on certain days listed within a registered calendar (such as business holidays)
- Repeated a specific number of times
- Repeated until a specific time/date
- Repeated indefinitely
- Repeated with a delay interval

Jobs are given names by their creator and can also be organized into named groups. Triggers may also be given names and placed into groups, to easily organize them within the scheduler. Jobs can be added to the scheduler once, but they can also be registered with multiple triggers.

Job execution

Here are the scenarios for job execution:

- Jobs can be any .NET class that implements the simple `IJob` interface, leaving infinite possibilities for the work that jobs can perform.
- Job class instances can be instantiated by Quartz.NET, or by your application's framework.
- When a trigger occurs, the scheduler notifies zero or more .NET objects implementing the `JobListener` and `TriggerListener` interfaces. These listeners are also notified after the job has executed.
- As jobs are completed, they return a `JobCompletionCode` that informs the scheduler of success or failure. `JobCompletionCode` can also instruct the scheduler of any actions it should take, based on the success/fail code, such as immediate re-execution of the job.

Job persistence

- The design of Quartz.NET includes an `IJobStore` interface that can be implemented to provide various mechanisms for the storage of jobs
- With the use of the included `AdoJobStore`, all jobs and triggers configured as **non-volatile** are stored in a relational database via **ADO.NET**
- With the use of the included `RAMJobStore`, all jobs and triggers are stored in RAM and therefore do not persist between program executions but this has the advantage of not requiring an external database

Clustering

Some of the benefits that clustering offers are:

- Failover
- Load balancing

Listeners and plugins

Listeners and plugins are a central component of Quartz.Net and here is why:

- Applications can catch scheduling events to monitor or control job/trigger behavior by implementing one or more listener interfaces
- The plugin mechanism can be used to add functionality to Quartz, such as keeping a history of job executions, or loading job and trigger definitions from a file
- Quartz ships with several factory built plugins and listeners

As you can see, there are many positive benefits to using Quartz, but one that I forgot to mention is stability. The best scheduler is kind of like the best logging tool: the best one is the one that you never realize is working. That sums up Quartz.NET perfectly; it just keeps on ticking.

Installing Quartz.NET server as a service

To install Quartz.NET, here is the ZIP file that you will need to download:

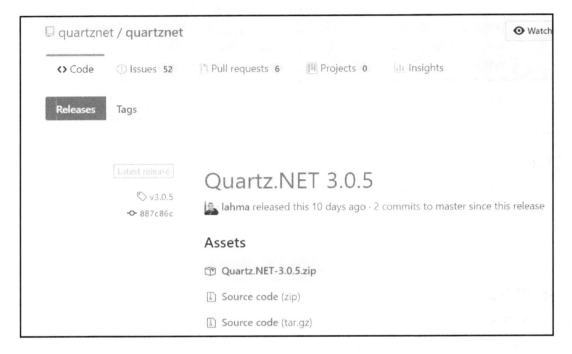

Unzip the package to your local hard drive:

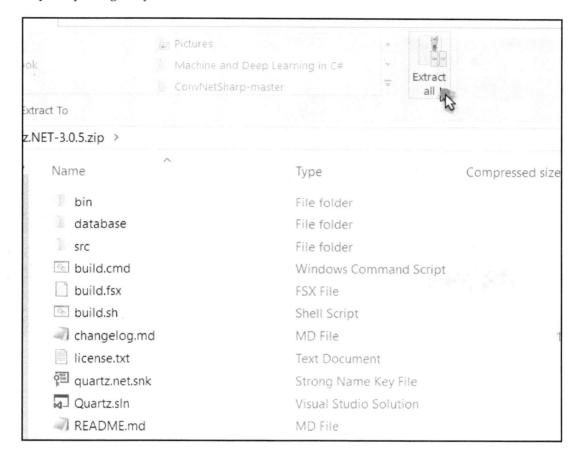

Install the server:

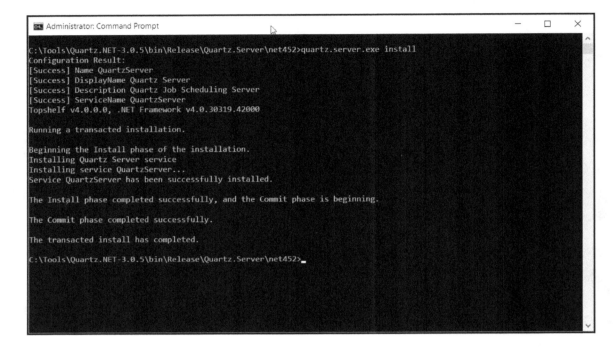

Verify that the installation was successful:

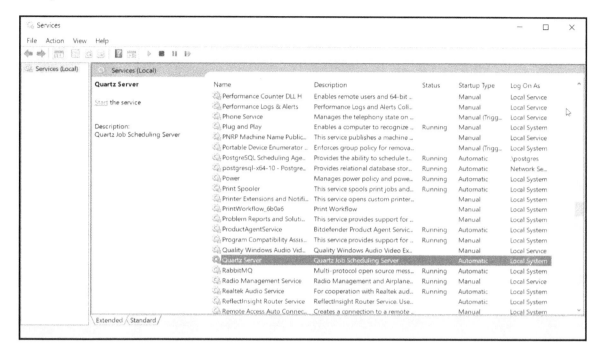

You can see the service properties once the service is properly installed:

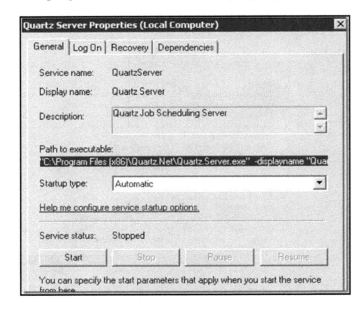

Our program

Here is what our `main.cs` looks like when completed. You will notice that this is quite different from the other main files we have created in that we are also dealing with the Quartz scheduler as well:

```
static void Main(string[] args)
{
var builder = new ContainerBuilder();
// Service itself
builder.RegisterType<SchedulingMicroService>()
.AsImplementedInterfaces()
.AsSelf()
?.InstancePerLifetimeScope();
builder.RegisterType<Logger>().SingleInstance();
var container = builder.Build();
XmlConfigurator.ConfigureAndWatch(new FileInfo(@".log4net.config"));
HostFactory.Run(c =>
{
c?.UseAutofacContainer(container);
c?.UseLog4Net();
```

```
c?.ApplyCommandLineWithDebuggerSupport();
c?.EnablePauseAndContinue();
c?.EnableShutdown();
c?.OnException(ex => { Console.WriteLine(ex.Message); });

// Here is the main difference in this Microservice. We are going to run
the Quartz scheduler as a microservice. We create our sample job, have it
run every 30 seconds until we stop the microservice.

c.ScheduleQuartzJobAsService(q =>
q.WithJob(() => JobBuilder.Create<SampleJob>().Build())
.AddTrigger(() => TriggerBuilder.Create().WithSimpleSchedule(
build => build.WithIntervalInSeconds(30).RepeatForever()).Build())
).StartAutomatically();
c?.Service<SchedulingMicroService>(s =>
{
s.ConstructUsingAutofacContainer<SchedulingMicroService>();
s?.ConstructUsing(settings =>
{
var service =
AutofacHostBuilderConfigurator.LifetimeScope.Resolve<SchedulingMicroService
>();
return service;
});
s?.ConstructUsing(name => new SchedulingMicroService());
s?.WhenStarted((SchedulingMicroService server, HostControl host) =>
server.OnStart(host));
s?.WhenPaused(server => server.OnPause());
s?.WhenContinued(server => server.OnResume());
s?.WhenStopped(server => server.OnStop());
s?.WhenShutdown(server => server.OnShutdown());
});
c?.RunAsNetworkService();
c?.StartAutomaticallyDelayed();
c?.SetDescription(string.Intern("Scheduling Microservice Sample"));
c?.SetDisplayName(string.Intern("SchedulingMicroService"));
c?.SetServiceName(string.Intern("SchedulingMicroService"));
c?.EnableServiceRecovery(r =>
{
r?.OnCrashOnly();
r?.RestartService(1); //first
r?.RestartService(1); //second
r?.RestartService(1); //subsequents
r?.SetResetPeriod(0);
});
});
}
```

The highlighted lines are the difference with this microservice. We are starting Quartz.NET up as a service, adding a job and a trigger, configuring the execution frequency of the job, and then telling Topshelf to start the process automatically. You would need to remove this section if you were going to start a job programmatically when you receive a message. But for now, this microservice is designed to know what it needs to do automatically, and to do that once it starts up. Both scenarios may work for you, and you ultimately may choose to have both kinds of microservices (one that accepts messages and one that does not) running in your ecosystem.

OnStart

Let's take a look at our `OnStart` method:

```
public new bool OnStart([CanBeNull] HostControl host)
{
base.Start(host);
_hc = host;
_jobScheduler?.Start();
//_logger?.SendInformation(string.Intern("Job scheduler started"));
// construct a scheduler factory
ISchedulerFactory schedFact = new StdSchedulerFactory();
// get a scheduler
IScheduler sched = schedFact.GetScheduler().Result;
sched.Start();
// define the job and tie it to our HelloJob class
IJobDetail job = JobBuilder.Create<SampleJob>()
.WithIdentity("myJob", "group1")
.Build();
// Trigger the job to run now, and then every 40 seconds
ITrigger trigger = TriggerBuilder.Create()
.WithIdentity("myTrigger", "group1")
.StartNow()
.WithSimpleSchedule(x => x
.WithIntervalInSeconds(40)
.RepeatForever())
.Build();
// Schedule the job
sched.ScheduleJob(job, trigger);
return true;}
```

What exactly are we doing here? Let's take it one step at a time:

1. The first line we encounter is to instantiate the scheduler from the factory
2. The second highlighted line starts the job scheduler

3. The third highlighted line creates a job for the system to run and identifies the job with a group
4. The fourth line creates a trigger for the group
5. The last line schedules the job based upon the trigger

And what does our scheduled job look like? It's about as simple as you could imagine, which makes me think that this is going to be a good exercise for you to enhance. All it does now is print out the time every time it is triggered, which is every 40 seconds:

```
public class SampleJob : IJob
{
public Task Execute(IJobExecutionContext context)
{
Console.WriteLine("The current time is: {0}",
SystemClock.Instance.GetCurrentInstant().ToDateTimeUtc().ToLocalTime());
return Task.CompletedTask;
}
}
```

All that we have to do, as `IJob` implementors, is to implement the `Execute` method and execute whatever program logic we deem necessary. Since the call is asynchronous, we need to return a `Task` to the caller. In our case, since this is such a simple method, we will just return `CompletedTask`. Let's look at a more complicated job:

```
class HelloWorldJob : IJob
{
private static readonly ILog Log =
LogManager.GetLogger(typeof(HelloWorldJob));
public HelloWorldJob()
{
}
[NotNull]
public Task Execute([NotNull] IJobExecutionContext context)
{
try
{
Console.WriteLine("{0}****{0}Job {1} fired @ {2} next scheduled for
{3}{0}***{0}",
Environment.NewLine, context.JobDetail?.Key,
context.FireTimeUtc.LocalDateTime.ToString("r"),
context.NextFireTimeUtc?.ToString("r"));
Console.WriteLine("{0}***{0}Hello World!{0}***{0}", Environment.NewLine);
}
catch (Exception ex)
{
Log?.DebugFormat("{0}***{0}Failed: {1}{0}***{0}", Environment.NewLine,
```

```
ex.Message);
}
return Task.CompletedTask;
}
}
```

Scheduling multiple jobs

So this is all nice and good, but what if we want or need to schedule multiple jobs at the same time? In our real world, that possibility is very high. Here's an example of doing just that:

```
HostFactory.Run(c =>
{
c.Service<ContainerService>(s =>
{
s.ConstructUsing(name => new ContainerService());
s.WhenStarted((service, control) => service.Start());
s.WhenStopped((service, control) => service.Stop());
s.ScheduleQuartzJob<ContainerService>(q =>
q.WithJob(() =>
JobBuilder.Create<JobA>().Build())
.AddTrigger(() =>
TriggerBuilder.Create()
.WithSimpleSchedule(builder => builder
.WithIntervalInSeconds(10)
.RepeatForever())
.Build())
);
s.ScheduleQuartzJob<ContainerService>(q =>
q.WithJob(() =>
JobBuilder.Create<JobB>().Build())
.AddTrigger(() =>
TriggerBuilder.Create()
.WithSimpleSchedule(builder => builder
.WithIntervalInSeconds(60)
.RepeatForever())
.Build())
);
});
});
```

Running our microservice

Even though the implementation is minimal, we are executing a scheduled job every 40 seconds. In your environment, you may have the need to execute one or more jobs on a periodic basis, but more than likely you will have a need to dynamically schedule something or execute a job as a result of another process. So, if your machine learning microservice (oops, early spoiler alert!) fails, you can stop the process and send an alert email or trigger a specific failure job that is defined to handle things when any microservice fails:

Summary

In this chapter, we discussed the great open source framework, Quartz.NET. We talked about how we schedule jobs, how we respond to scheduled jobs, and what we do once our job is triggered. We developed a microservice that can run scheduled jobs, and now the only thing that you need to do is go through the chapter exercises and make it your own! In our next chapter, we are going to continue our separation of concerns strategy and develop an email management microservice. Fun times await!

Exercises

1. Send email messages to the microservice
2. Process incoming email requests the way you need
3. Implement multiple schedules if needed

7
Designing an Email Microservice

Inevitably, there will come a time when our application will have to log messages, send an email, or both. In this chapter, we will be discussing the latter, sending emails. The sending of emails fits in perfectly with the microservice architecture guidelines that we laid out earlier. It is extremely business-specific, self-contained, adheres to separation of concerns, and is self-deployable.

In this chapter, we will learn the following:

- How to send emails based upon a message subscription
- How to send emails without knowing the SMTP host

Installation

We will start by creating a **Console App (.NET Framework)**, as we have done for all of our other microservices. I know at times it may seem redundant to provide the same information over and over, but keep in mind that there really is no recommended chapter reading order for this book. Users should feel free to skip to sections that interest them. By showing specific details, even if it's identical to other chapters, this prevents the reader from having to read the book in order. I hope that made sense!

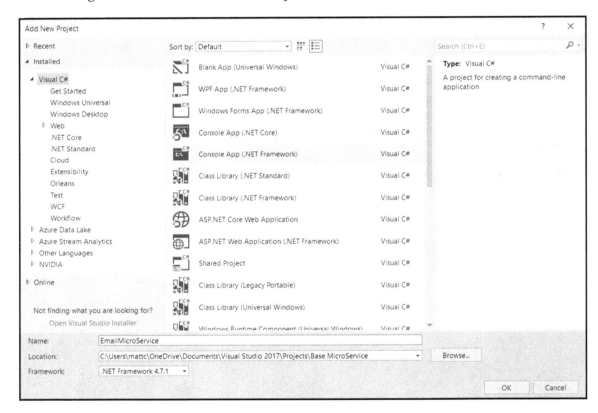

Once completed, we will have the same basic template as our other microservices. Let's see what it looks like when it is complete.

Our program

The following is the code from our `main.cs` method. As you can see, it follows the paradigm of all the other chapters. By now, this code should have become somewhat, if not totally, familiar to you.

The code does the following:

- Builds our **Autofac** container
- Registers our types and interfaces
- Configures all of our **Topshelf** parameters
- Provides all events
- Tells our microservice how to handle failures
- Runs our main email microservice

Here is our `main.cs` function block:

```
static void Main(string[] args)
{
var builder = new ContainerBuilder();
builder.RegisterType<Logger>()?.SingleInstance();
builder.RegisterType<EmailMS>()
.AsImplementedInterfaces()
.AsSelf()
?.InstancePerLifetimeScope();
var container = builder.Build();
XmlConfigurator.ConfigureAndWatch(new FileInfo(@".log4net.config"));
HostFactory.Run(c =>
{
c?.UseAutofacContainer(container);
c?.UseLog4Net();
c?.ApplyCommandLineWithDebuggerSupport();
c?.EnablePauseAndContinue();
c?.EnableShutdown();
c?.OnException(ex => Console.WriteLine(ex.Message));
c?.Service<EmailMS>(s =>
{
s.ConstructUsingAutofacContainer<EmailMS>();
s?.ConstructUsing(settings =>
{
var service =
AutofacHostBuilderConfigurator.LifetimeScope.Resolve<EmailMS>();
return service;
});
s?.ConstructUsing(name => new EmailMS());
```

```
s?.WhenStarted((EmailMS server, HostControl host) => server.OnStart(host));
s?.WhenPaused(server => server?.OnPause());
s?.WhenContinued(server => server?.OnResume());
s?.WhenStopped(server => server?.OnStop());
s?.WhenShutdown(server => server?.OnShutdown());
});
c?.RunAsNetworkService();
c?.StartAutomaticallyDelayed();
c?.SetDescription(string.Intern("Email MicroService Sample"));
c?.SetDisplayName(string.Intern("EmailMicroService"));
c?.SetServiceName(string.Intern("HealthMonitoringMicroService"));
c?.EnableServiceRecovery(r =>
{
r?.OnCrashOnly();
r?.RestartService(1); //first
r?.RestartService(1); //second
r?.RestartService(1); //subsequents
r?.SetResetPeriod(0);
});
});
}
```

OnStart

Since our microservice is an example, we use the OnStart message to trigger the sending
of an email. In the real world, you would want to do this based upon an event or action
occurrence. I will leave it up to you, the reader and developer, as you know what works
best with your environment. Regardless of your approach, it's an easy enhancement to
make:

```
public new bool OnStart([CanBeNull] HostControl host)
{
Start(host);
Subscribe();
EmailSendRequest m = new EmailSendRequest();
m.Subject = "Test";
m.To = "noone@gmail.com";
m.From = "nobody@nowhere.com";
m.Body = "This is a test of the email microservice system";
SendEmail(m);
return true;
}
```

In the preceding code, we call the base `Start` method, subscribe to our message system, and send an email. Please note, before I get any nasty emails, that the preceding email addresses are completely, totally, and irrevocably incorrect. Please don't paste the code and tell me the email isn't working. You will know who you are sending an email `To` and what you want the `From` to look like. These few lines of code are where you can make the greatest positive impact to your microservice.

Subscribing to messages

In order to send or receive messages, we have to be subscribed to our underlying messaging system. You will notice that, to do this, we call the `Subscribe` method. You'll also notice that this is another one of those sections that gets repeated a lot, for the same reasons as stated previously. But this is also one of the great candidates to be put into our base class for everyone to use. At the time of writing, it was not included in the base class source code, but I would take a look anyway, I might have been able to sneak in a few goodies between draft and final!

The following code does the following:

- Creates our connection to the RabbitMQ server
- Enables message versioning
- Declares our exchanges
- Declares our email queue
- Binds our `queue` to the `exchange`
- Subscribes to our `EmailSendRequest` message and provides the function to call once the message is received

Here is our subscribe function which will handle declaring and binding Exchanges and Queues, as well as subscribing to messages:

```
public void Subscribe()
{
Bus = RabbitHutch.CreateBus("host=localhost",
x =>
{
x.Register<IConventions, AttributeBasedConventions>();
x.EnableMessageVersioning();
});
IExchange exchange = Bus.Advanced.ExchangeDeclare("EvolvedAI",
ExchangeType.Topic);
IQueue queue = Bus.Advanced.QueueDeclare("Email");
```

```
Bus.Advanced.Bind(exchange, queue, Environment.MachineName);
Bus.Subscribe<EmailSendRequest>(Environment.MachineName, msg => {
ProcessEmailSendRequestMessage(msg); },
config => config?.WithTopic("Email"));
}
```

The preceding highlighted lines are the code that is specific to us. More concretely, the highlighted code subscribes to, and processes, EmailSendReceipt messages for us. These few lines of code are where all the magic happens.

Processing messages

When we receive a request to send an email, we will be receiving an EmailSendRequest message. That message should be fully populated with all of the information we need to send the email. In the following code, our ProcessEmailSendRequestMessage is triggered as soon as we receive a request message. From there, we will pass the message to our SendMessage function to handle sending the email:

```
bool ProcessEmailSendRequestMessage(EmailSendRequest msg)
{
Console.WriteLine("Received Email Send Request Message");
RILogManager.Default?.SendInformation("Received Email Send Request
Message");
SendEmail(msg);
return true;
}
```

Now that the framework of our microservice is complete, let's create a routine that will send an email, but we're going to do it with a twist. Let's see if you can figure out what is happening differently.

Here's how we send a simple message. Before looking at it, I want to point out that for those wanting to learn and for those with a creative spirit, this might be the most individually customized, influenced object we deal with in the entire book. You can absolutely explode with creative ideas of how to create fancy or professional looking emails, how to substitute in previously designed email templates, and much more:

```
EmailSendRequest m = new EmailSendRequest();
m.Subject = "Test";
m.To = "noone@gmail.com";
m.From = "nobody@nowhere.com";
m.Body = "This is a test of the email microservice system";
Console.WriteLine(EmailSender.Send(m.From, m.To, m.Subject, m.Body)
? "Email sent" : "Email not sent");
```

And here's our `Send` function:

```
public static bool Send(string from, string to, string subject, string
body)
{
string domainName = GetDomainName(to);
IPAddress[] servers = GetMailExchangeServer(domainName);
foreach (IPAddress server in servers)
{
try
{
SmtpClient client = new SmtpClient(server.ToString(), SmtpPort);
client.Send(from, to, subject, body);
return true;
}
catch
{
continue;
}
}
return false;
}
```

Can you see yet what it is that we are doing differently compared with probably every other `email.send` routine you've done? If not, think harder. Notice that the `SmtpClient` constructor and `Send` calls are embedded inside a `for` loop. This `for` loop is going to enumerate over every possible server IP address for mail exchanges until either one works, or until we have completed without success.

Internally, we have our `FindDnsServers` function, and its job is to get the domain server for our email address by checking the registry and returning all the values. The probability that one of them will work is very high, and this way we don't have to do the normal `SmtpClient` initialization and provide usernames and passwords.

Finding DNS servers

One of the (admittedly) harder ways of knowing your SMTP server is to check the Windows registry for the correct keys. But if you don't know your SMTP host, or it isn't working for you, then you now have an alternative:

DNS entries are stored in the Windows registry. The following code goes to the registry and retrieves a list of named servers for each entry. That server list is then returned to the caller, and each server will be substituted for the SMTP hostname you would normally provide, and the sending of the email is attempted until successful:

```
public static string[] FindDnsServers()
{
RegistryKey start = Registry.LocalMachine;
string DNSservers = @"SYSTEMCurrentControlSetServicesTcpipParameters";
RegistryKey DNSserverKey = start.OpenSubKey(DNSservers);
if (DNSserverKey == null)
{
return null;
}
string serverlist = (string)DNSserverKey.GetValue("NameServer");
DNSserverKey.Close();
start.Close();
if (string.IsNullOrWhiteSpace(serverlist))
{
return null;
}
string[] servers = serverlist.Split(' ');return servers;
}
```

Subscribing to email requests

Here's our code that we use to subscribe to our `EmailSendRequest` messages. Once we receive one we will immediately process this via the `ProcessEmailSendRequestMessage` function:

```
public void Subscribe()
{
Bus = RabbitHutch.CreateBus("host=localhost",
x => x.Register<IConventions, AttributeBasedConventions>());
IExchange exchange = Bus.Advanced.ExchangeDeclare("EvolvedAI",
ExchangeType.Topic);
IQueue queue = Bus.Advanced.QueueDeclare("Email");
Bus.Advanced.Bind(exchange, queue, Environment.MachineName);
Bus.Subscribe<EmailSendRequest>(Environment.MachineName, msg => {
ProcessEmailSendRequestMessage(msg); },
config => config?.WithTopic("Email"))
}
```

This in turn, calls our internal `SendEmail` function, passes the message with all the required parameters, and then sends the message:

```
bool ProcessEmailSendRequestMessage(EmailSendRequest msg)
{
Console.WriteLine("Received Email Send Request Message");
RILogManager.Default?.SendInformation("Received Email Send Request
Message");
SendEmail(msg);
return true;
}
```

Did you notice that when we subscribe to a message this time, we are specifically looking for an exact topic, in this case, `Email`? `WithTopic` extensions will be a great help moving forward in subscribing to our intended messages.

Once this is complete, our message will have been sent and received.

Summary

To truly focus on separation of concerns, having a separate email sending microservice is critical. Many microservices may need to accomplish this task after completion or upon error, and the last thing that we want to do is duplicate code. The more duplicate code, the greater the chance for error! In our next chapter, we will be developing a file monitoring microsystem that will help you monitor file and directory changes.

Exercises

Here are some exercises for your consideration:

1. Widen the email message request so that it can take all fields within an SMTP message
2. Send an email confirmation response to the requestor of the email
3. Make sure the email is HTML and add HTML code to the body and subject

8
Designing a File Monitoring Microservice

One of the many uses of a microservice is to monitor changes in a filesystem. Files being dropped to an FTP site, text files containing data to be processed, files to archive, the list goes on and on. Most file and directory changes in corporate America will more than likely be those arriving from external vendors to someone in your company, and usually comprise many files coming in and going out on a daily basis. This could be pricing feeds, vendor data uploads, and so on. What if we were to automate what happened when files are received, and the reverse of that, as a result of some action or command, we could also send a file out?

In this chapter, we are going to:

- Build a file monitoring microservice
- Show you how to modify this microservice so that you can mold it into your own based upon the files and directories that you need to monitor

Overview of FileSystemWatcher

As C# developers, you may already be familiar with the Windows `FileSystemWatcher` object and its capabilities. Before we get into writing our `FileSystemWatcher`, let's talk a little bit about how Windows and you, as a C# developer, handle monitoring changes to the filesystem.

The `FileSystemWatcher` object in .NET is the object that you will use to monitor a filesystem. Like most other input and output items, it is in the `System.IO` namespace. The filesystem monitor allows you to monitor directories and file types for changes. You can use it to watch for changes to a specific directory, files and subdirectories of a specific directory, and you can do so on a local computer, remote computer, or networked drive.

You do this by supplying a filter to the watcher so it knows the types of files to monitor for. In many cases, this can be the * . * wildcard.

Alongside the filter, there are several types of changes that you can watch for. They are as follows:

Member name	Description
Attributes	The attributes of the file or folder
CreationTime	The time the file or folder was created
DirectoryName	The name of the directory
FileName	The name of the file
LastAccess	The date the file or folder was last opened
LastWrite	The date the file or folder last had anything written to it
Security	The security settings of the file or folder
Size	The size of the file or folder

As well as files, we can also tell filewatcher to monitor subdirectories underneath the folder we are monitoring. This is helpful if your file management approach has, say, a folder for every vendor for instance.

Once a file event happens, the filewatcher object needs to know what to do. This happens by assigning event handlers to several predefined watcher events. The predefined events are:

- File changed
- File created
- File deleted
- File renamed

At the time of writing, there were some known issues with the filewatcher. They are:

- Hidden files are not ignored.
- In some systems, FileSystemWatcher reports changes to files using the short 8.3 filename format. For example, a change to LongFileName.LongExtension could be reported as LongFil~.Lon.

- This class contains a link demand and an inheritance demand at the class level that applies to all members. A security exception is thrown when either the immediate caller or the derived class does not have full-trust permission.
- The maximum size you can set for the `InternalBufferSize` property for monitoring a directory over the network is 64 KB.

Internal buffer

The `FileSytemWatcher` component uses an internal buffer to keep track of filesystem actions. By default, the buffer is set to a size of 4 KB. A 4 KB buffer can track changes on approximately 80 files in a directory. Each event takes up 16 bytes in the buffer, plus enough bytes to store the name of the file, in Unicode (two bytes per character), that the event occurred on. You can use this information to approximate the buffer size you will need. You reset the buffer size by setting the `InternalBufferSize` property.

Why are we talking about this? Because if there are many changes in a short time, the buffer can overflow. This causes the component to lose track of changes in the directory, and will affect correct notification. Increasing the size of the buffer is expensive, as it comes from non-paged memory that cannot be swapped out to disk, so we must keep the buffer as small as possible. Setting the filter does not decrease what goes into the buffer. If you are using Microsoft Windows 2000, you should increase the buffer size in increments of 4 KB, because this corresponds to the operating system's default page size. With any other operating system, you should increase the buffer size in increments that correspond to the operating system's default page size. If you are unsure of the default page size for the operating system you are using, the safest way to proceed is to just double the original size of the buffer. This will maintain the original interval needed for your operating system.

In this chapter, I will present two solutions for file watching for you. You can choose the style you like most. The first will wrap the Windows `FileSystemWatcher` object into two unique and helpful classes. The second will be more aggressive in reducing the number of events raised through the system. Why do I mention this?

For those who have worked with the Windows `FileSystemWatcher` object before, you know that one file action on your part can result in many events being generated. You think there should just be one created event, but, in fact, several `Created`, `Changed`, and `Renamed` events are possible. Something like this you would never expect unless you worked with it. Here's an example of what I mean.

Excel triggers 15 NTFS events for four different files when creating a single new .xlsx file and triggers eight events for three different files, of which none is a changed event for the file change one would naively expect. Just take a look at what is really happening behind the scenes:

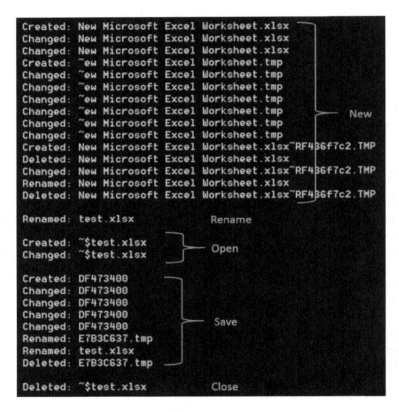

Excel triggering events

Building your microservice – part one

In our first example, we are going to manually wrap the Windows FileSystemWatcher object to do what we want. This will give us ultimate control over the object and the process. This work was originally done by Mr. Peter Meinl, and a big thanks goes out to him to allow us to use his work in this book. You can check out his blog at https://petermeinl.wordpress.com/.

Here's what we hope to accomplish in this chapter:

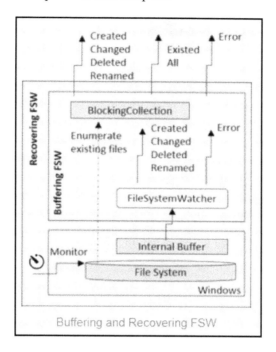

Architecture of classes: Buffering and Recovering FSW

The first class we will provide is the `BufferingFileSystemWatcher`. This object:

- Buffers `FileSystemWatcher` events in a `BlockingCollection`. This helps reduce memory consumption and it even over increases the internal buffer size.
- Reports existing files via a new event, `Existed`.
- Provides sorting events by oldest (existing) files first. This is the default when subscribing to the `All` or `Existing` events.
- Provides an `All` event. This helps reduce time and effort in subscribing to all events.
- Wraps the `FileSystemWatcher` via composition so its API is not broken. This then offers a direct drop-in replacement for `FileSystemWatcher`.

The following listing shows key parts of the `BufferingFileSystemWatcher`:

```
public class BufferingFileSystemWatcher : Component
{
private FileSystemWatcher _containedFSW = null;
```

```
...
public BufferingFileSystemWatcher()
{
_containedFSW = new FileSystemWatcher();
}
...
public bool EnableRaisingEvents
{
get
{
return _containedFSW.EnableRaisingEvents;
}
set
{
if (_containedFSW.EnableRaisingEvents == value) return;
StopRaisingBufferedEvents();
_cancellationTokenSource = new CancellationTokenSource();
_containedFSW.EnableRaisingEvents = value;
if (value) RaiseBufferedEventsUntilCancelled();
}
}
...
public event FileSystemEventHandler All
{
add
{
if (_onAllChangesHandler == null)
{
_containedFSW.Created += BufferEvent;
_containedFSW.Changed += BufferEvent;
_containedFSW.Renamed += BufferEvent;
_containedFSW.Deleted += BufferEvent;
}
_onAllChangesHandler += value;
}
...
private void BufferEvent(object _, FileSystemEventArgs e)
{
if (!_fileSystemEventBuffer.TryAdd(e))
{
var ex = new EventQueueOverflowException($"Event queue size
{_fileSystemEventBuffer.BoundedCapacity} events exceeded.");
InvokeHandler(_onErrorHandler, new ErrorEventArgs(ex));
}
}
...
private void RaiseBufferedEventsUntilCancelled()
{
```

```
Task.Run(() =>;
{
try
{
if (_onExistedHandler != null || _onAllChangesHandler != null)
NotifyExistingFiles();
foreach (FileSystemEventArgs e in
_fileSystemEventBuffer.GetConsumingEnumerable(_cancellationTokenSource.Toke
n))
{
if (_onAllChangesHandler != null)
InvokeHandler(_onAllChangesHandler, e);
else
{
switch (e.ChangeType)
{
case WatcherChangeTypes.Created:
InvokeHandler(_onCreatedHandler, e);
break;
case WatcherChangeTypes.Changed:
InvokeHandler(_onChangedHandler, e);
break;
case WatcherChangeTypes.Deleted:
InvokeHandler(_onDeletedHandler, e);
break;
case WatcherChangeTypes.Renamed:
InvokeHandler(_onRenamedHandler, e as RenamedEventArgs);
break;
catch (OperationCanceledException)
{ } //ignore
catch (Exception ex)
{
BufferingFileSystemWatcher_Error(this, new ErrorEventArgs(ex));
private void NotifyExistingFiles()
{
if (OrderByOldestFirst)
{
var searchSubDirectoriesOption = (IncludeSubdirectories) ?
SearchOption.AllDirectories : SearchOption.TopDirectoryOnly;
var sortedFileNames = from fi in new DirectoryInfo(Path).GetFiles(Filter,
searchSubDirectoriesOption)
orderby fi.LastWriteTime ascending
select fi.Name;
foreach (var fileName in sortedFileNames)
{
InvokeHandler(_onExistedHandler, new
FileSystemEventArgs(WatcherChangeTypes.All, Path, fileName));
InvokeHandler(_onAllChangesHandler, new
```

```
FileSystemEventArgs(WatcherChangeTypes.All, Path, fileName));
}
}
else
{
foreach (var fileName in Directory.EnumerateFiles(Path))
{
InvokeHandler(_onExistedHandler, new
FileSystemEventArgs(WatcherChangeTypes.All, Path, fileName));
InvokeHandler(_onAllChangesHandler, new
FileSystemEventArgs(WatcherChangeTypes.All, Path, fileName));
...
```

The second object I will provide you with is the `RecoveringFileSystemWatcher`. Why use this class? Well, just a few of the reasons are as follows:

- Detects and reports watch path accessibility problems. Using a poll timer monitoring the watch path and the `FileSystemWatcher` error event. For robustness, restarting from the `Error` event is not done directly, but it is also done via the timer!
- Automatically recovers from watch path accessibility problems by restarting the `BufferingFileSysteWatcher`. New files created during the outage are reported via the `Existed` event.
- Allows consumers to cancel auto recovery for selected exceptions using `e.Handled=True`.

The following listing shows key parts of the `RecoveringFileSystemWatcher`:

```
public class RecoveringFileSystemWatcher : BufferingFileSystemWatcher
{
public TimeSpan DirectoryMonitorInterval = TimeSpan.FromMinutes(5);
public TimeSpan DirectoryRetryInterval = TimeSpan.FromSeconds(5);
private System.Threading.Timer _monitorTimer = null;
...

// Our property for raising events
public new bool EnableRaisingEvents
{
get { return base.EnableRaisingEvents; }
set
{
if (value == EnableRaisingEvents) return;
base.EnableRaisingEvents = value;
if (EnableRaisingEvents)
{
```

```
base.Error += BufferingFileSystemWatcher_Error;
Start();
}
else
{
base.Error -= BufferingFileSystemWatcher_Error;
}

// Start our file watcher
private void Start()
{
try
{
_monitorTimer = new System.Threading.Timer(_monitorTimer_Elapsed);
Disposed += (_, __) =>;
{
_monitorTimer.Dispose();
_trace.Info("Obeying cancel request");
};
ReStartIfNeccessary(TimeSpan.Zero);

// Our timer event
private void _monitorTimer_Elapsed(object state)
{
try
{
if (!Directory.Exists(Path))
{
throw new DirectoryNotFoundException($"Directory not found {Path}");
}
else
{
_trace.Info($"Directory {Path} accessibility is OK.");
if (!EnableRaisingEvents)
{
EnableRaisingEvents = true;
if (_isRecovering)
_trace.Warn("<== Watcher recovered");
}
ReStartIfNeccessary(DirectoryMonitorInterval);
}
}
catch (Exception ex) when (
ex is FileNotFoundException
|| ex is DirectoryNotFoundException)
{
if (ExceptionWasHandledByCaller(ex))
return;
```

```
if (_isRecovering)
{
_trace.Warn("...retrying");
}
else
{
_isRecovering = true;
}
EnableRaisingEvents = false;
_isRecovering = true;
ReStartIfNeccessary(DirectoryRetryInterval);
}
catch (Exception ex)
{
_trace.Error($"Unexpected error: {ex}");
throw;
private void ReStartIfNeccessary(TimeSpan delay)
{
try
{
_monitorTimer.Change(delay, Timeout.InfiniteTimeSpan);
}
catch (ObjectDisposedException)
{ } //ignore timer disposed
}

// This is our error event
private void BufferingFileSystemWatcher_Error(object sender, ErrorEventArgs
e)
{
var ex = e.GetException();
if (ExceptionWasHandledByCaller(e.GetException()))
return;
EnableRaisingEvents = false;
if (ex is InternalBufferOverflowException || ex is
EventQueueOverflowException)
{
ReStartIfNeccessary(DirectoryRetryInterval);
}
\else if (ex is Win32Exception && (ex.HResult ==
NetworkNameNoLongerAvailable | ex.HResult == AccessIsDenied))
ReStartIfNeccessary(DirectoryRetryInterval);
}
```

Here is `RecoveringFileSystemWatcher` in action:

```
48:56,387|  Start: Will auto-detect unavailability of watched directory.
            - Windows timeout accessing network shares: ~110 sec on start,
              ~45 sec while watching.
48:56,408|  _monitorTimer_Elapsed: Watching:\\gogo\test\in
? Processing...  |Press <Enter> to contine.
48:56,476|  _monitorTimer_Elapsed: Directory \\gogo\test\in accessibility is OK.
48:56,480|  ProcessFile: 04.05.2015 09:48:56 -Polled- \\gogo\test\in\Test-1.xml
49:06,223|  ProcessFile: 04.05.2015 09:49:06 -Created- \\gogo\test\in\Test-2.xml
49:46,501|  _fileWatcher_Error: The specified network name is no longer available
49:46,503|  _fileWatcher_Error: Will try to recover automatically!
49:51,506|  _monitorTimer_Elapsed: Watching:\\gogo\test\in
51:00,036|  _monitorTimer_Elapsed: => Directory \\gogo\test\in Is Not accessible.
            - Will try to recover automatically in 00:00:05!
51:05,038|  _monitorTimer_Elapsed: Watching:\\gogo\test\in
51:05,052|  _monitorTimer_Elapsed: ...retrying
51:10,055|  _monitorTimer_Elapsed: Watching:\\gogo\test\in
51:10,078|  _monitorTimer_Elapsed: ...retrying
51:15,080|  _monitorTimer_Elapsed: Watching:\\gogo\test\in
51:15,094|  _monitorTimer_Elapsed: ...retrying
51:20,096|  _monitorTimer_Elapsed: Watching:\\gogo\test\in
51:20,109|  _monitorTimer_Elapsed: ...retrying
51:25,110|  _monitorTimer_Elapsed: Watching:\\gogo\test\in
51:25,123|  _monitorTimer_Elapsed: ...retrying
51:30,125|  _monitorTimer_Elapsed: Watching:\\gogo\test\in
51:30,178|  _monitorTimer_Elapsed: Directory \\gogo\test\in accessibility is OK.
51:30,183|  ProcessFile: 04.05.2015 09:51:30 -Polled- \\gogo\test\in\Test-3.xml
51:30,183|  _monitorTimer_Elapsed: <= Watcher recovered
51:37,231|  ProcessFile: 04.05.2015 09:51:37 -Created- \\gogo\test\in\Test-4.xml
51:42,672|  _Lambda$__22-0: Obeying cancel request
Stopping...
? Stopped.  |Press <Enter> to contine.
```

RecoveringFileSystemWatcher working and auto recovering

We will put both of these objects to work in our first example, the
`AdvancedFileMonitoringMicro`. As with all our other microservices, we need to create a
Console App (.NET Framework) as follows:

With our base project created, we need to complete our `main.cs` file. Here's what it looks
like completed:

```
static void Main(string[] args)
{
Console.WindowWidth = 130;
var builder = new ContainerBuilder();
// Service itself
builder.RegisterType<MSBaseLogger>()?.SingleInstance();
builder.RegisterType<Microservice>()
.AsImplementedInterfaces()
.AsSelf()
?.InstancePerLifetimeScope();
_container = builder.Build();
```

```
XmlConfigurator.ConfigureAndWatch(new FileInfo(@".log4net.config"));
HostFactory.Run(c =>
{
c?.UseAutofacContainer(_container);
c?.UseLog4Net();
c?.EnablePauseAndContinue();
c?.EnableShutdown();
c?.Service<Microservice>(s =>
{
s.ConstructUsingAutofacContainer<Microservice>();
s?.ConstructUsing(settings =>
{
var service =
AutofacHostBuilderConfigurator.LifetimeScope.Resolve<Microservice>();
return service;
});
s?.ConstructUsing(name => new Microservice(_container,
Guid.NewGuid().ToString()));
s?.WhenStartedAsLeader(b =>
{
b.WhenStarted(async (service, token) =>
{
await service.Start(token);
});
b.Lease(lcb => lcb.RenewLeaseEvery(TimeSpan.FromSeconds(2))
.AquireLeaseEvery(TimeSpan.FromSeconds(5))
.LeaseLength(TimeSpan.FromDays(1))
.WithLeaseManager(new Microservice()));
b.WithHeartBeat(TimeSpan.FromSeconds(30), (isLeader, token) =>
Task.CompletedTask);
b.Build();
});
s?.WhenStarted((Microservice server, HostControl host) =>
server.OnStart(host));
s?.WhenPaused(server => server?.OnPause());
s?.WhenContinued(server => server?.OnResume());
s?.WhenStopped(server => server?.OnStop());
s?.WhenShutdown(server => server?.OnShutdown());
s?.WhenCustomCommandReceived((server, host, code) => { });
s?.AfterStartingService(() => { });
s?.AfterStoppingService(() => { });
s?.BeforeStartingService(() => { });
s?.BeforeStoppingService(() => { });
});
c?.RunAsNetworkService();
c?.StartAutomaticallyDelayed();
c?.SetDescription(string.Intern("Advanced File Watching Sample"));
c?.SetDisplayName(string.Intern("AdvancedFileWatchingMicroservice"));
```

```
c?.SetServiceName(string.Intern("AdvancedFileWatchingMicroservice"));
c?.EnableServiceRecovery(r =>
{
r?.OnCrashOnly();
r?.RestartService(1); //first
r?.RestartService(1); //second
r?.RestartService(1); //subsequents
r?.SetResetPeriod(0);
});
});
}
```

Making sure our message queue and exchange are created

The following code creates our connection to RabbitMQ, creates the exchange and the queue, and binds both:

```
private void Subscribe()
{
Bus = RabbitHutch.CreateBus("host=localhost",
x =>
{
x.Register<IConventions, AttributeBasedConventions>();
x.EnableMessageVersioning();
});
IExchange exchange = Bus?.Advanced?.ExchangeDeclare("EvolvedAI",
ExchangeType.Topic);
IQueue queue = Bus?.Advanced?.QueueDeclare("FileSystem");
Bus?.Advanced?.Bind(exchange, queue, "");
}
```

Our OnStart method for this microservice is very similar to other microservices you have seen, with the addition of the highlighted line. This line actually runs the recovering filewatcher for us:

```
public new bool OnStart([CanBeNull] HostControl host)
{
Host = host;
Name = "Microservice Manager_" + Environment.MachineName;
Start(host);
Subscribe();
using (var scope = _container?.BeginLifetimeScope())
{
```

```
var logger = scope?.Resolve<MSBaseLogger>();
logger?.LogInformation(Name + " Microservice Starting");
}
const double interval = 60000;
_timer = new Timer(interval);
_timer.Elapsed += OnTick;
_timer.AutoReset = true;
_timer.Start();
RunRecoveringWatcher();
return true;
}
```

Running the recovery filewatcher

Our recovery filewatcher is run via a method of the same name. Within the function, we will respond to the various events in place. For each event we will display the message to the console output and then create and post a filesystem message with the results:

```
void RunRecoveringWatcher()
{
Console.WriteLine("Will auto-detect unavailability of watched directory");
Console.WriteLine(" - Windows timeout accessing network shares: ~110 sec on
start, ~45 sec while watching.");
using (var watcher = new RecoveringFileSystemWatcher(TestPath))
{
watcher.All += (_, e) => { WriteLineInColor($"{e.ChangeType} {e.Name}",
ConsoleColor.Yellow); };
watcher.Error += (_, e) =>
{
WriteLineInColor(e.Error.Message, ConsoleColor.Red);
};
watcher.Existed += (_, e) =>
{
WriteLineInColor($"Existed {e.Name}", ConsoleColor.Yellow);
};
watcher.Created += (_, e) =>
{
WriteLineInColor($"Created {e.Name}", ConsoleColor.Yellow);
FileSystemChangeMessage m = new FileSystemChangeMessage
{
ChangeDate =
SystemClock.Instance.GetCurrentInstant().ToDateTimeUtc().ToLocalTime(),
ChangeType = (int)e.ChangeType,
FullPath = e.FullPath,
Name = e.Name
};
```

```
_bus.Publish(m, "FileSystemChanges");
};
watcher.Deleted += (_, e) =>
{
WriteLineInColor($"Deleted {e.Name}", ConsoleColor.Yellow);
FileSystemChangeMessage m = new FileSystemChangeMessage
{
ChangeDate =
SystemClock.Instance.GetCurrentInstant().ToDateTimeUtc().ToLocalTime(),
ChangeType = (int)e.ChangeType,
FullPath = e.FullPath,
Name = e.Name
};
_bus.Publish(m, "FileSystemChanges");
};
watcher.Renamed += (_, e) =>
{
WriteLineInColor($"Renamed {e.OldName} to {e.Name}", ConsoleColor.Yellow);
FileSystemChangeMessage m = new FileSystemChangeMessage
{
ChangeDate =
SystemClock.Instance.GetCurrentInstant().ToDateTimeUtc().ToLocalTime(),
ChangeType = (int)e.ChangeType,
FullPath = e.FullPath,
OldPath = e.OldFullPath,
Name = e.Name,
OldName = e.OldName
};
_bus.Publish(m, "FileSystemChanges");
};
watcher.Changed += (_, e) =>
{
WriteLineInColor($"Changed {e.Name}", ConsoleColor.Yellow);
FileSystemChangeMessage m = new FileSystemChangeMessage
{
ChangeDate =
SystemClock.Instance.GetCurrentInstant().ToDateTimeUtc().ToLocalTime(),
ChangeType = (int)e.ChangeType,
FullPath = e.FullPath,
Name = e.Name
};
_bus.Publish(m, "FileSystemChanges");
};
watcher.DirectoryMonitorInterval = TimeSpan.FromSeconds(10);
watcher.OrderByOldestFirst = false;
watcher.DirectoryRetryInterval = TimeSpan.FromSeconds(5);
watcher.IncludeSubdirectories = false;
//watcher.EventQueueCapacity = 1;
```

```
watcher.EnableRaisingEvents = true;
PromptUser("Processing...");
Console.WriteLine("Stopping...");
}
PromptUser("Stopped.");
}
```

Building your microservice – part two

In the second half of our chapter, we will create another `FileSystemWatcher` for you, but this time we'll approach it a bit differently. As with all our other microservices, the first thing we need to do is create our console application. In this instance, we will name it `FileSystemMonitorMicroService` as follows:

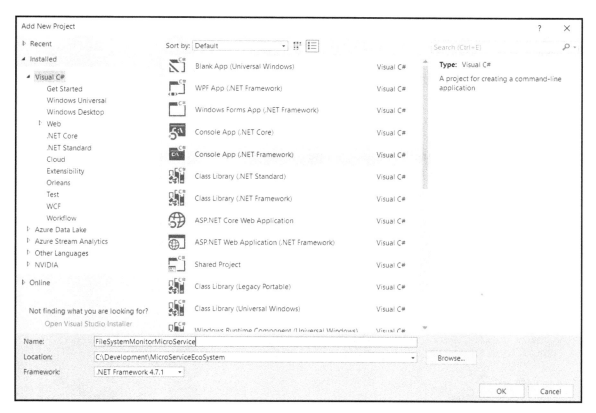

With that being done, and our template project in place, we now need to add the NuGet package, `Topshelf.FileSystemWatcher`. This is a very simple, yet powerful, library that is specifically designed to monitor filesystem change events on Windows and will save us a lot of work from writing our own.

Here's what it looks like from within NuGet:

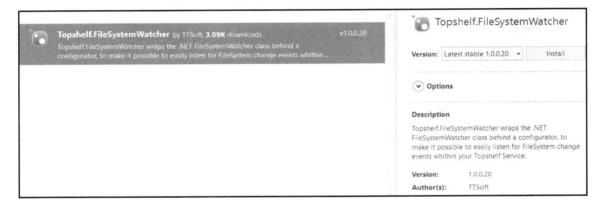

Our message

The following is what our filesystem change message looks like. Once we receive a filesystem event, we will populate and send this message to whomever is listening for it:

```
/// <summary> (Serializable) a file system change message. </summary>
[Serializable]
[Queue("FileSystem", ExchangeName = "EvolvedAI")]
public class FileSystemChangeMessage
{
public int ChangeType { get; set; }
public int EventType { get; set; }
public DateTime ChangeDate { get; set; }
public string FullPath { get; set; }
public string OldPath { get; set; }
public string Name { get; set; }
public string OldName { get; set; }
}
```

Building our main program

Now that everything is in place, let's start building our microservice. We will start by adding three variables we need to keep track of. The first is the name of the directory we should monitor for changes. This will be a directory called `test` located directly under our executing assembly directory:

```
private static readonly string _testDir = Directory.GetCurrentDirectory() +
@"test";
```

The second variable will track if we want to monitor subdirectories for changes as well:

```
private static readonly bool _includeSubDirectories = true;
```

As an example, we might have a main (`testDir`) called `Incoming` and one called `Outgoing`, and underneath would be subdirectories for the vendors that we use. Our filesystem might look something like the following:

Our third variable is perhaps the most helpful in that it prevents us from supplying duplicate events to the user. For those that have written filewatchers before, you know that many duplicate events can be triggered when files are created, especially the larger they are. This next variable helps us manage that:

```
private static readonly bool _excludeDuplicateEvents = true;
```

Notes on events

The following are some notes on **gotcha** points with filesystem events that you should be aware of:

- Common filesystem operations may raise more than one event. For example, when a file is moved from one directory to another, several OnChanged and some OnCreated and OnDeleted events might be raised. Moving a file is a complex operation that consists of multiple simple operations, therefore raising multiple events. Likewise, some applications (for example, antivirus software) might cause additional filesystem events that are detected by the watcher.
- The watcher can watch disks if they are not switched or removed. The watcher does not raise events for CDs and DVDs because time stamps and properties cannot change. Remote computers must have one of the required platforms installed for the component to function properly.
- If multiple watcher objects are watching the same UNC path in Microsoft Windows XP prior to **Service Pack 1 (SP1)**, or Windows 2000 SP2 or earlier, then only one of the objects will raise an event. On machines running Microsoft Windows XP SP1 and newer, Windows 2000 SP3 or newer, or Windows Server 2003, all watchers will raise the appropriate events.

With that out of the way, we need to now write our main program.cs file. It will be the same as all our others, but with some very special additions:

```
private static void Main(string[] args)
{
HostFactory.Run(config =>
{
config.Service<Program>(s =>
{
s.ConstructUsing(() => new Program());
s.BeforeStartingService((hostStart) =>
{
CreateTopology("EvolvedAI", "FileSystemChanges");
if (!Directory.Exists(_testDir))
Directory.CreateDirectory(_testDir);
});
s.WhenStarted((service, host) => true);
s.WhenStopped((service, host) => true);
s.WhenFileSystemCreated(ConfigureDirectoryWorkCreated, FileSystemCreated);
s.WhenFileSystemChanged(ConfigureDirectoryWorkChanged, FileSystemCreated);
s.WhenFileSystemRenamed(ConfigureDirectoryWorkRenamedFile,
FileSystemRenamedFile);
s.WhenFileSystemRenamed(ConfigureDirectoryWorkRenamedDirectory,
```

```
FileSystemRenamedDirectory);
s.WhenFileSystemDeleted(ConfigureDirectoryWorkDeleted, FileSystemCreated);
});
});
Console.ReadKey();
}
```

As you can see with the preceding highlighted code, we have highlighted the sections on this main module that are specific to `FileSystemWatcher`. You will notice that there are event handlers for files created, changed, renamed, deleted, and directories renamed.

Now let's look at the handlers themselves. There is one for each event we handle. The main point to notice is that when an event occurs, we gather all the information and publish a message for anyone who is listening:

```
private static void FileSystemCreated(
  TopshelfFileSystemEventArgs
  topshelfFileSystemEventArgs)
{
//Here we create our change message
FileSystemChangeMessage m = new FileSystemChangeMessage
{
```

Note that we are not using `DateTime.Now` here, but the `NodaTime` instant. This ensures consistent time throughout the entire ecosystem when events are reported and/or logged:

```
ChangeDate =
SystemClock.Instance.GetCurrentInstant().ToDateTimeUtc().ToLocalTime(),
ChangeType = (int)topshelfFileSystemEventArgs.ChangeType,
EventType = (int)topshelfFileSystemEventArgs.FileSystemEventType,
FullPath = topshelfFileSystemEventArgs.FullPath,
OldPath = topshelfFileSystemEventArgs.OldFullPath,
Name = topshelfFileSystemEventArgs.Name,
OldName = topshelfFileSystemEventArgs.OldName
};
```

Here we publish our message:

```
PublishMessage(m, "EvolvedAI", "");
Console.WriteLine("********************");
Console.WriteLine("ChangeType = {0}",
topshelfFileSystemEventArgs.ChangeType);
Console.WriteLine("FullPath = {0}", topshelfFileSystemEventArgs.FullPath);
Console.WriteLine("Name = {0}", topshelfFileSystemEventArgs.Name);
Console.WriteLine("FileSystemEventType {0}",
topshelfFileSystemEventArgs.FileSystemEventType);
Console.WriteLine("********************");
```

```
}
private static void FileSystemRenamedFile(
  TopshelfFileSystemEventArgs
  topshelfFileSystemEventArgs)
{
FileSystemChangeMessage m = new FileSystemChangeMessage
{
ChangeDate =
SystemClock.Instance.GetCurrentInstant().ToDateTimeUtc().ToLocalTime(),
ChangeType = (int)topshelfFileSystemEventArgs.ChangeType,
EventType = (int)topshelfFileSystemEventArgs.FileSystemEventType,
FullPath = topshelfFileSystemEventArgs.FullPath,
OldPath = topshelfFileSystemEventArgs.OldFullPath,
Name = topshelfFileSystemEventArgs.Name,
OldName = topshelfFileSystemEventArgs.OldName
};
PublishMessage(m, "EvolvedAI", "");
Console.WriteLine("*********************");
Console.WriteLine("Rename File");
Console.WriteLine("ChangeType = {0}",
topshelfFileSystemEventArgs.ChangeType);
Console.WriteLine("FullPath = {0}", topshelfFileSystemEventArgs.FullPath);
Console.WriteLine("Name = {0}", topshelfFileSystemEventArgs.Name);
Console.WriteLine("FileSystemEventType {0}",
topshelfFileSystemEventArgs.FileSystemEventType);
Console.WriteLine("*********************");
}
private static void FileSystemRenamedDirectory(
  TopshelfFileSystemEventArgs
  topshelfFileSystemEventArgs)
{
FileSystemChangeMessage m = new FileSystemChangeMessage
{
ChangeDate =
SystemClock.Instance.GetCurrentInstant().ToDateTimeUtc().ToLocalTime(),
ChangeType = (int)topshelfFileSystemEventArgs.ChangeType,
EventType = (int)topshelfFileSystemEventArgs.FileSystemEventType,
FullPath = topshelfFileSystemEventArgs.FullPath,
OldPath = topshelfFileSystemEventArgs.OldFullPath,
Name = topshelfFileSystemEventArgs.Name,
OldName = topshelfFileSystemEventArgs.OldName
};
PublishMessage(m, "EvolvedAI", "");
Console.WriteLine("*********************");
Console.WriteLine("Rename Dir");
Console.WriteLine("ChangeType = {0}",
topshelfFileSystemEventArgs.ChangeType);
Console.WriteLine("FullPath = {0}", topshelfFileSystemEventArgs.FullPath);
```

```
Console.WriteLine("Name = {0}", topshelfFileSystemEventArgs.Name);
Console.WriteLine("FileSystemEventType {0}",
topshelfFileSystemEventArgs.FileSystemEventType);
Console.WriteLine("*********************");
}
```

This is what our application looks like when it is running, and we drop files into our `test` directory:

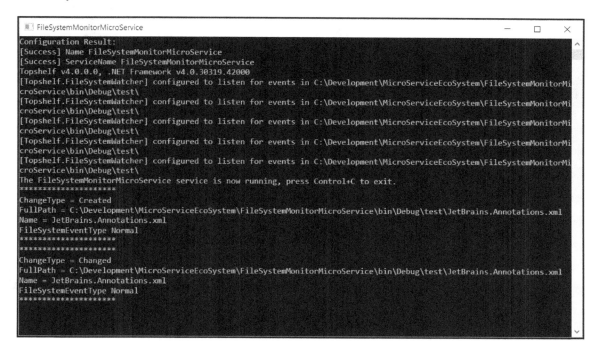

Here is another screenshot that shows memory profiling messages being processed:

```
MicroServiceManager                                             —    □    ×
Memory Used: 52.0 MB
*** Memory at ***Saturday, June 2, 2018 8:34:26 AM
        Memory before GC: 5.38 MB
CPU Used: 24.0450344085693
        Memory after GC: 2.42 MB
        App memory being used: 52.0 MB
                Generation 0 Collection Count: 7
                Generation 1 Collection Count: 5
Message: OK
                Time Spent in GC: 00.01%
*** Memory ***
Received Memory Update Message
Heartbeat
Received Health Status Message
Service: Microservice Manager_EVOLVEDAI
Status: 1
Microservice Manager_EVOLVEDAI Reclaiming Memory
Memory Used: 51.9 MB
*** Memory at ***Saturday, June 2, 2018 8:35:26 AM
        Memory before GC: 3.35 MB
CPU Used: 7.50879335403442
        Memory after GC: 2.43 MB
        App memory being used: 51.9 MB
                Generation 0 Collection Count: 9
                Generation 1 Collection Count: 7
Message: OK
                Time Spent in GC: 03.52%
*** Memory ***
Received Memory Update Message
```

Summary

In this chapter, we have learned about the Windows `FileSystemWatcher` object and how it works. We created a custom file watching microservice that will respond to file change events and publish them for other microservices to consume. We also talked about some of the things to watch out for when it comes to events and buffers. Finally, we showed you a great open source project that abstracts all the work of writing `FileSystemWatcher`.

In the next chapter we will develop the internals of a machine learning Microservice from which you can expand to meet your needs.

Exercises

Here are some exercises for your consideration:

1. Modify the filewatcher to watch the subdirectories most important to you

Creating a Machine Learning Microservice

9

Machine learning is everywhere nowadays. But do you think you can turn machine learning into a microservice? Of course we can! We can execute all of the instructions, which are distinct calls we make in our machine learning application, and send and process them via messages. We can then make the final result available to anyone that wants it, an instant microservice!

In this chapter, we will learn the following:

- How to create a microservice that can implement machine learning techniques
- How to use the ConvNet open source framework
- How to expand this example to meet your particular needs

Installation

Our machine learning microservice will be a **Console App (.NET Framework)**, just as all our other microservices have been:

Additionally, we are going to use another great open source framework, `ConvNetSharp`. There are two `.dll` files that must be referenced, and these are as follows. Without these, the machine won't be learning! You could have just as easily referenced a NuGet package, but I figured we're far enough along in the book and we know each other enough that we can mix it up a bit:

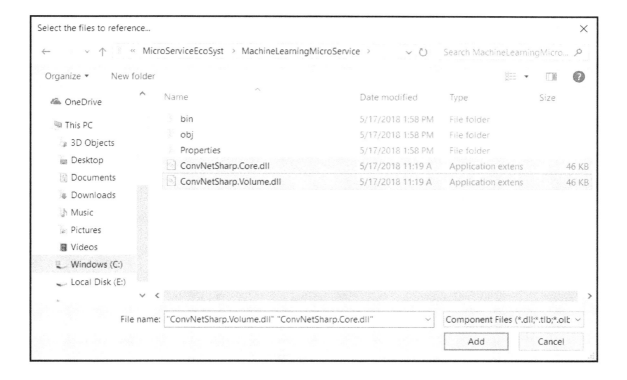

Our program

With our `main.cs` file filled out, here's how it will look. As this is a microservice that may run multiple instances for performance reasons when training the network, I have added leadership capabilities via `Topshelf.Leader`. I have highlighted the relevant sections of code that pertain to this:

```
static void Main(string[] args)
{
var builder = new ContainerBuilder();
// Service itself
builder.RegisterType<MLMicroService>()
.AsImplementedInterfaces()
.AsSelf()
?.InstancePerLifetimeScope();
builder.RegisterType<Logger>().SingleInstance();
var container = builder.Build();
XmlConfigurator.ConfigureAndWatch(new FileInfo(@".log4net.config"));
HostFactory.Run(c =>
```

```
{
c?.UseAutofacContainer(container);
c?.UseLog4Net();
c?.ApplyCommandLineWithDebuggerSupport();
c?.EnablePauseAndContinue();
c?.EnableShutdown();
c?.OnException(ex => { Console.WriteLine(ex.Message); });
c?.UseWindowsHostEnvironmentWithDebugSupport();
c?.Service<MLMicroService>(s =>
{
s.ConstructUsingAutofacContainer<MLMicroService>();
s?.ConstructUsing(settings =>
{
var service =
AutofacHostBuilderConfigurator.LifetimeScope.Resolve<MLMicroService>();
return service;
});
s?.ConstructUsing(name => new MLMicroService());
s?.WhenStartedAsLeader(b =>
{
b.WhenStarted(async (service, token) =>
{
await service.Start(token);
});
b.Lease(lcb => lcb.RenewLeaseEvery(TimeSpan.FromSeconds(2))
.AquireLeaseEvery(TimeSpan.FromSeconds(5))
.LeaseLength(TimeSpan.FromDays(1))
.WithLeaseManager(new MLMicroService()));
b.WithHeartBeat(TimeSpan.FromSeconds(30), (isLeader, token) =>
Task.CompletedTask);
b.Build();
});
s?.WhenStarted((MLMicroService server, HostControl host) =>
server.OnStart(host));
s?.WhenPaused(server => server.OnPause());
s?.WhenContinued(server => server.OnResume());
s?.WhenStopped(server => server.OnStop());
s?.WhenShutdown(server => server.OnShutdown());
});
c?.RunAsNetworkService();
c?.StartAutomaticallyDelayed();
c?.SetDescription(string.Intern("Machine Learning Microservice Sample"));
c?.SetDisplayName(string.Intern("MachineLearningMicroservice"));
c?.SetServiceName(string.Intern("MachineLearningMicroService"));
c?.EnableServiceRecovery(r =>
{
r?.OnCrashOnly();
r?.RestartService(1); //first
```

```
r?.RestartService(1); //second
r?.RestartService(1); //subsequents
r?.SetResetPeriod(0);
});
});
}
```

For this microservice, we have our message titled MLMessage. This message takes a different turn from previous messages in that it allows for four parameters, two reply values and two reply messages. You see, we really don't know what is going to be required each step of the way. Each step in training or configuring our machine learning microservice takes different parameters and produces different results. By leaving our message definition flexible, we put the onus on the caller for populating parameters correctly, and then the implementor of our microservice to interpret them together. Consider it a contract between developers, not classes. Our MLMessage looks as follows:

```
[Serializable]
[Queue("MachineLearning", ExchangeName = "EvolvedAI")]
public class MLMessage
{
public int MessageType { get; set; }
public int LayerType { get; set; }
public double param1 { get; set; }
public double param2 { get; set; }
public double param3 { get; set; }
public double param4 { get; set; }
public double replyVal1 { get; set; }
public double replyVal2 { get; set; }
public string replyMsg1 { get; set; }
public string replyMsg2 { get; set; }
}
```

Moving on from the message, let's take a look at what makes our OnStart method unique. The highlighted lines, of which there are many, are publishing configuration messages to the machine learning microservice. Once all the parameters are created properly, the network is trained and our results are published. Normally, this code would not go here. I only put it here so that as soon as the microservice starts (the same applies with other microservices in the book), it immediately sends out a message relative to what it does. I will leave it as an exercise to you, the reader, to put this in its proper place and call it when and how required.

When we are finished, our CNN will look as follows:

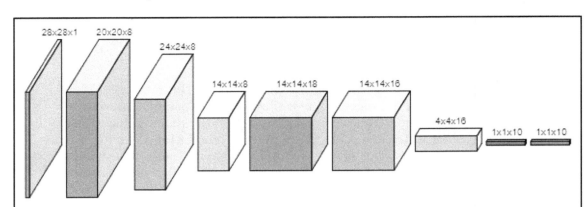

OnStart

Our `OnStart` method is much more complex than previous microservices, but again this is for education purposes only. As you can see, the `OnStart` method actually sends all the messages required to build and train the network. In production-level code you may or may not do this, but just in case, I have highlighted the sections of code that pertain to building and training the neural network:

```
public new bool OnStart([CanBeNull] HostControl host)
{
Host = host;
base.Start(host);
CreateNetwork();
Subscribe("MachineLearning", "", (msg) => { ProcessMLMessage(msg, null);
});
Console.WriteLine(string.Intern("Machine Learning MicroService Started."));
```

1. Declare the first layer as an input layer. Since we are using two-dimensional data, we do not care about the three-dimensional volume (tensor) that we maintain (width, height, depth). We will therefore set the width and height to a size of one:

```
PublishMessage("EvolvedAI", "", MLMessageType.AddLayer,
LayerType.InputLayer, 1,1,2,"test1","test2", string.Empty);
```

2. Declare a layer with 20 neurons:

```
PublishMessage("EvolvedAI", "", MLMessageType.AddLayer,
LayerType.FullyConnLayer, 20, 0, 0, string.Empty, string.Empty,
string.Empty);
```

3. Declare a **Rectified Linear Unit (ReLU)**:

```
PublishMessage("EvolvedAI", "", MLMessageType.AddLayer,
LayerType.ReluLayer, 0, 0, 0, string.Empty, string.Empty,
string.Empty);
```

4. Declare a fully-connected layer that will be used by the SoftmaxLayer:

```
PublishMessage("EvolvedAI", "", MLMessageType.AddLayer,
LayerType.FullyConnLayer, 10, 0, 0, string.Empty, string.Empty,
string.Empty);
```

5. Declare the linear classifier on top of the previously hidden layer:

```
PublishMessage("EvolvedAI", "", MLMessageType.AddLayer,
LayerType.SoftmaxLayer, 10, 0, 0, string.Empty, string.Empty,
string.Empty);
```

6. Forward a random data point through the network:

```
PublishMessage("EvolvedAI", "", MLMessageType.Forward,
LayerType.None, 0.3, -0.5, 2, string.Empty, string.Empty,
string.Empty);
```

7. Our result is a volume (tensor). They have weight properties that store the raw data, and weight gradients that store gradients:

```
PublishMessage("EvolvedAI", "", MLMessageType.GetResult,
LayerType.None, 0.3, -0.5, 2, string.Empty, string.Empty,
string.Empty);
return (true);
}
```

Processing a machine learning request

Once a machine learning request has been processed and a reply message is available, we want to consume it right away. We will know of the completion because the performing microservice will be responsible for sending a response/completion message so that others may know of the status.

Here is our `ProcessMLMessage` function that will handle the incoming message. Depending upon the message type, it will display the appropriate information:

```
bool ProcessMLMessage([NotNull] MLMessage msg, [NotNull]
MessageReceivedInfo mri)
{
Console.WriteLine("Received Machine Learning Message");
RILogManager.Default?.SendInformation("Received Machine Learning Message");
switch ((MLMessageType)msg.MessageType)
{
```

1. Add a `LayerType` type of layer to the ConvNet:

```
case MLMessageType.AddLayer:
RILogManager.Default?.SendInformation("Adding a layer command");
CreateLayer((LayerType)msg.LayerType, msg.param1, msg.param2,
msg.param3);
PublishMessage("EvolvedAI", "", MLMessageType.Reply,
LayerType.None, 0, 0,0,"Success", "", "");
break;
```

2. Create the network and all the variables in it:

```
case MLMessageType.Create:
RILogManager.Default?.SendInformation("Create command");
CreateNetwork();
PublishMessage("EvolvedAI", "", MLMessageType.Reply,
LayerType.None, 0, 0, 0, "Success", "", "");
break;
```

3. Make the network start to work:

```
case MLMessageType.Forward:
RILogManager.Default?.SendInformation("Forward command");
ForwardPoint(msg.param1, msg.param2, msg.param3);
PublishMessage("EvolvedAI", "", MLMessageType.Reply,
LayerType.None, 0, 0, 0, "Success", "", "");
break;
```

4. Get the final result of the test:

```
case MLMessageType.GetResult:
RILogManager.Default?.SendInformation("Requesting Results");
PublishMessage("EvolvedAI", "", MLMessageType.Reply,
LayerType.None, _probability, 0, 0,
"probability that x is class 0: " + _probability.Get(0), "", "");
break;
```

5. Train the network:

```
case MLMessageType.Train:
RILogManager.Default?.SendInformation("Training the network");
TrainNetwork(msg.param1, msg.param2, msg.param3, msg.param4);
PublishMessage("EvolvedAI", "", MLMessageType.Reply,
LayerType.None, 0, 0, 0, "Success", "", "");
break;
```

6. Answer back:

```
case MLMessageType.Reply:
Console.WriteLine(msg.replyMsg1);
Console.WriteLine(msg.replyMsg2);
break;
}
return true;
}
```

Creating a layer

There are several types of layers that our neural network can create. Since for this example we are dealing with a CNN, the first layer must be a fully convolutional layer. The first layer to be added must be an input layer or an exception will be thrown. After the input layer is added, the next layer must be a classification layer. This is a fully connected layer with a defined neuronal count, bias, bias gradient, bias preference values, and L1 and L2 decay multipliers. If the layer is a ReLU layer, ReLU nonlinearity element wise will be implemented such that $x \rightarrow max(0,x)$, with the output being zero to infinity.

Creating a network

There are three ways to programmatically create a neural network with this open source package:

- Core layers:
    - Mo computational graph
    - Network organized by stacking layers

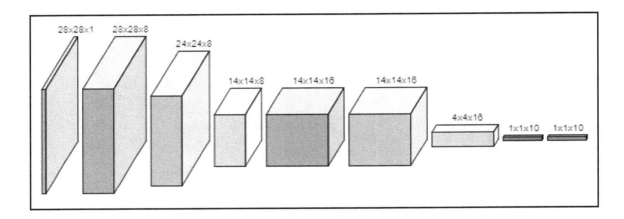

- Flow layers:
    - Layers that create a computational graph behind the scenes
    - Network organized by stacking layers

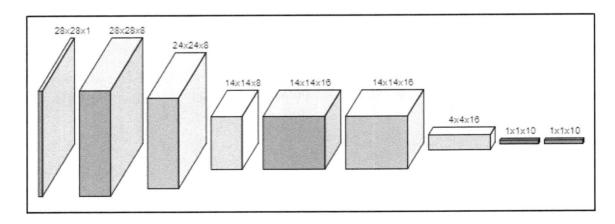

- Computational graph:
    - Pure flow.
    - Operations connected to each other. Can implement more complex networks.

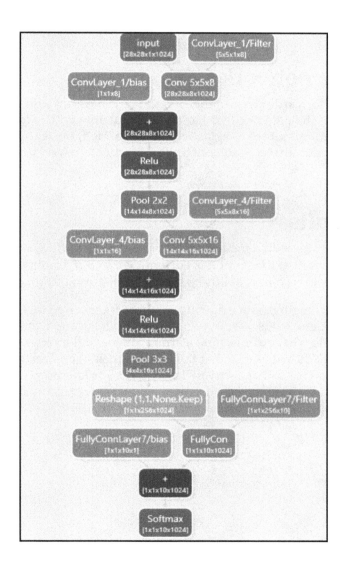

Traversing the forward path through the network

Executing the MLMessage type of Forward will forward a random data point through the network. It will start at layer zero and work its way through to the last layer. The result of this will be a volume, more commonly referred to in some circles as a tensor. Volumes have weight properties that store the raw data, and weight gradients that store the gradients.

Training the network

Training will make a forward pass and then a backward pass through the network, traversing all layers of the network. The lists of accumulators will be initialized in the first iteration. An update for all sets of weights will be performed, the learning rate and momentum updated, the correct gradient applied, gradients zeroed out, and then the process repeated.

Getting results

Publishing an MLMessage with a message type of GetResult will get the volume (tensor) probability of the network at the point it is currently at. In our example at the start of the chapter, this should give us a probability of somewhere around *0.501*.

With the machine learning messages flowing, we now move on to take a look at what our RabbitMQ message queue looks like. If we are lucky, and we are, we will have message traffic. The following is what our machine learning queue will look like once we begin processing messages. You will notice that there are **23** messages already in our queue. This tells us that we have no consumers actively looking for our microservice or the message level would be at zero because the microservice would have consumed all of the messages. So, if you see messages in your queue, much like water on your floor, something's wrong!

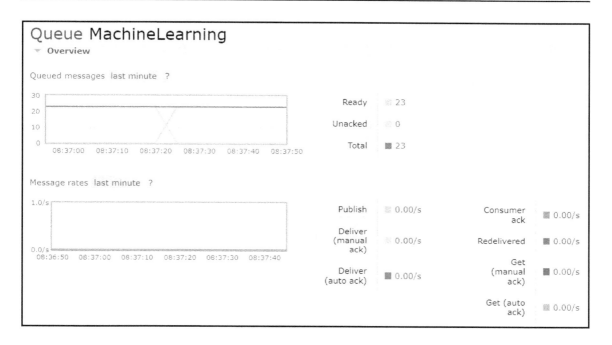

Summary

In this chapter, we created a machine learning microservice. We learned how to create a message flexible enough to accept a wide variety of parameters. We also created a neural network, trained it, and obtained the final results. The beauty of this is that there are so many open source frameworks that you could chose to integrate, and all you have to do is follow this simple approach and you're off!

In the next chapter we are going to develop a quantitative financial Microservice (Quant for short) and show you some fascinating things you can do with it.

10
Creating a Quantitative Financial Microservice

Quantitative finance: depending upon where you live, this may be an everyday requirement for you. Bigger cities and financial hubs, such as New York, Chicago, and London, will have this everywhere. But for those not familiar with the term, let's start with a brief description of what we are dealing with. Quantitative finance is a field of applied mathematics. It deals mostly with the modeling of financial markets. It overlaps heavily with computational finance and financial engineering, focusing on applications and modeling, as well as building tools for model implementation. The term most familiar with quantitative financing are the people that do it, more commonly referred to as **quants**. What does a quant do? Well, a financial economist will study structural relationships and the reasons why a corporation trades under a specific share price, while a quant will assume that the share price is a given and use mathematical techniques to elucidate the fair value of derivatives of the underlying stock.

In this chapter, we will cover the following:

- Creating a quantitative financial microservice
- Price bonds
- Price **Credit Default Swap (CDS)**

There is no doubt that in your particular situation you will need to hook up to a live information feed or other data source, and luckily you have the freedom to do just that. We will take the steps necessary to get you up and running using predefined values, and you can replace them with the pricing source of your choice. Let's start by creating our console application, as we did with our other microservices. We will call this microservice `QuantMicroService` for ease of use.

Installation

As usual, we will create a **Console App (.NET Framework)** for our microservice:

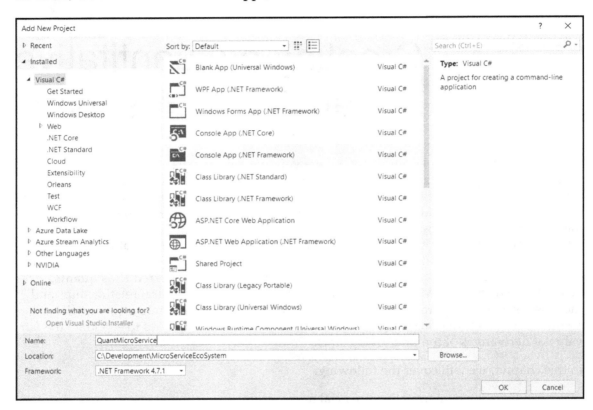

In this microservice, we will use an open source library to help us with the quant work. This library is QLNet.dll and you can find the source for it on GitHub at https://github. com/amaggiulli/QLNet. As we did in our Chapter 9, *Creating a Machine Learning Microservice* chapter, we are going to reference the **QuantLib** framework via .dll instead of the NuGet package. Again, you have the freedom to do whatever you like when you implement your full version:

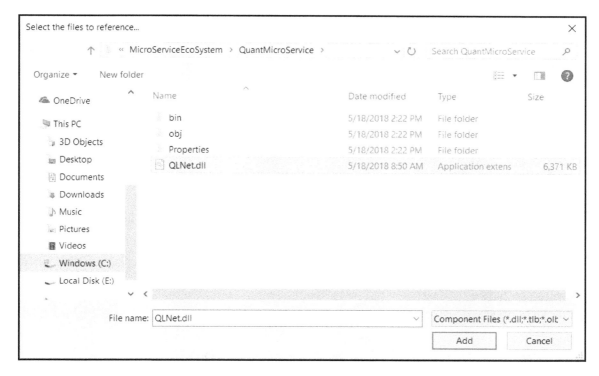

Once this library is installed, we are ready to go. In order to communicate throughout our system, we are going to have to create some common messages, just as we did for the other microservices. Let's start out with one for a CDS. A CDS is basically insurance, insurance against non-payment or a default on payments. If you remember, they were very prominent during the financial crisis of 2008.

We are going to have two messages per financial instrument this time: one for requests and one for responses. They will be identical in structure, so we will just show you the request message here. We are doing it this way to show you how we can receive a message and send a response with the same microservice. In fact, taking that one step further, we are sending both types of messages as well as listening for them. We will post a request message, receive it, process it, send a reply, receive the reply, and print out the results.

With our `main.cs` template provided, let's go ahead and fill it out completely. When we are done, it will look like this:

```
static void Main(string[] args)
{
var builder = new ContainerBuilder();
/ Service itself
```

```
builder.RegisterType<Logger>()?.SingleInstance();
builder.RegisterType<QuantMicroService>()
.AsImplementedInterfaces()
.AsSelf()
?.InstancePerLifetimeScope();
var container = builder.Build();
XmlConfigurator.ConfigureAndWatch(new FileInfo(@".log4net.config"));
HostFactory.Run(c =>
{
c?.UseAutofacContainer(container);
c?.UseLog4Net();
c?.ApplyCommandLineWithDebuggerSupport();
c?.EnablePauseAndContinue();
c?.EnableShutdown();
c?.OnException(ex => Console.WriteLine(ex.Message));
c?.Service<QuantMicroService>(s =>
{
s.ConstructUsingAutofacContainer<QuantMicroService>();
s?.ConstructUsing(settings =>
{
var service =
AutofacHostBuilderConfigurator.LifetimeScope.Resolve<QuantMicroService>();
return service;
});
s?.ConstructUsing(name => new QuantMicroService());
s?.WhenStarted((QuantMicroService server, HostControl host) =>
server.OnStart(host));
s?.WhenPaused(server => server?.OnPause());
s?.WhenContinued(server => server?.OnResume());
s?.WhenStopped(server => server?.OnStop());
s?.WhenShutdown(server => server?.OnShutdown());
});
c?.RunAsNetworkService();
c?.StartAutomaticallyDelayed();
c?.SetDescription(string.Intern("Quantitative Finance MicroService
Sample"));
c?.SetDisplayName(string.Intern("QuantFinanceMicroService"));
c?.SetServiceName(string.Intern("QuantFinanceMicroService"));
c?.EnableServiceRecovery(r =>
{
r?.OnCrashOnly();
r?.RestartService(1); //first
r?.RestartService(1); //second
r?.RestartService(1); //subsequents
r?.SetResetPeriod(0);
});
});
}
```

Our messages

For this microservice, we are going to create custom messages for bonds and for CDSs. The following code shows what they look like when completed. Notice that we use the `queue` attribute to make sure the end location of the message is correctly known—at least the `queue` and `exchange` parts anyways!

CDS-request message

This is how our `CreditDefaultSwapRequestMessage` looks. You can see that we use the `queue` and `exchange` attributes to direct our message to the correct `queue` and `exchange`:

```
[Queue("Financials", ExchangeName = "EvolvedAI")]
[Serializable]
public class CreditDefaultSwapRequestMessage
{
public double fixedRate { get; set; }
public double notional { get; set; }
public double recoveryRate {get; set;}
public double fairRate { get; set; }
public double fairNPV { get; set; }
}
```

Bonds request message

```
[Queue("Financial", ExchangeName = "EvolvedAI")]
[Serializable]
public class BondsRequestMessage
{
public DateTime issue { get; set; }
public DateTime maturity { get; set; }
public double coupon { get; set; }
public int frequency { get; set; }
public double yield { get; set; }
public string compounding { get; set; }
public double price { get; set; }
public double calcYield { get; set; }
public double price2 { get; set; }
public string message { get; set; }
}
```

Subscribing to messages

Our subscription to messages follows the same paradigm we've used in other microservices. We will:

1. Create our `Bus`
2. Create `exchange` and `queue`
3. Bind them together

The interesting thing about this microservice, which you will also see in the microservice manager, is that we are now subscribing to multiple messages instead of just one. The unique code is highlighted as follows:

```
public void Subscribe()
{
1.Bus = RabbitHutch.CreateBus("host=localhost",
x => x.Register<IConventions, AttributeBasedConventions>());
2. IExchange exchange = Bus.Advanced.ExchangeDeclare("EvolvedAI",
ExchangeType.Topic);
IQueue queue = Bus.Advanced.QueueDeclare("Financial");
3. Bus.Advanced.Bind(exchange, queue, "");

// functions to process subscription messages
Bus.Subscribe<CreditDefaultSwapRequestMessage>("CDSRequest", msg =>{
ProcessCDSMessage(msg); },
config => config.WithTopic("CDSRequest"));
Bus.Subscribe<CreditDefaultSwapResponseMessage>("CDSResponse", msgR => {
ProcessCDSResponse(msgR); },
config => config.WithTopic("CDSResponse"));
Bus.Subscribe<BondsRequestMessage>("BondRequest", msg => {
ProcessBondsMessage(msg); },
config => config.WithTopic("BondRequest"));
Bus.Subscribe<BondsResponseMessage>("BondResponse", msgR => {
ProcessBondsResponse(msgR); },
config => config.WithTopic("BondResponse"));}
```

1. Create our connection to the RabbitMQ service
2. Create our `exchange`
3. Create our `queue` and bind it to the `exchange`

The code highlighted is our request to process each message. We have four functions set up and ready to process messages: `ProcessCDSResponse`/request and `ProcessBondsResponse`/request.

Publishing our request message

The following is our `OnStart` method, and with it we are asking for both a CDS and a bond to be filled in with its relative information. The actual publish message lines are highlighted as follows. We first create each message, fill out the parameters of what we need to price our instruments, and publish the message to our `queue`. Please remember the actual financial instruments are for example only. You will need to fill in your specific information in order to achieve your results:

```
public bool OnStart([CanBeNull] HostControl host)
{
Start(host);
Subscribe();
CreditDefaultSwapRequestMessage msgT = new
CreditDefaultSwapRequestMessage();
msgT.fixedRate = 0.001;
msgT.notional = 10000.0;
msgT.recoveryRate = 0.4;
PublishRequestMessage(msgT, "CDSRequest");
BondsRequestMessage r = new BondsRequestMessage();
PublishBondRequestMessage(r, "BondRequest");
return true;
}
```

Now that we have published our request message, since we subscribed to it, we will receive the notification, and when we do, we will fill in the information similar to how you see it here. We have highlighted the line to where we now publish the response message. Remember, in your world, you are not going to be calling the methods like I am for illustration. Please use time from one of the chapter exercises for you to complete this process as suits your needs:

```
public bool ProcessCDSMessage(CreditDefaultSwapRequestMessage cds)
{
Create a CDS object.
CDS c = new CDS();

Calculate the Credit Default Swap
bool result = c.CalcCDS(ref cds, cds.fixedRate, cds.notional,
cds.recoveryRate);

// the message is populated with the fair rate and NPV now.
CreditDefaultSwapResponseMessage cd = new
CreditDefaultSwapResponseMessage();
cd.fixedRate = cds.fixedRate;
cd.fairNPV = cds.fairNPV;
cd.fairRate = cds.fairRate;
```

```
cd.notional = cds.notional;
cd.recoveryRate = cds.recoveryRate;

Publish the message
PublishResponseMessage(cd, "CDSResponse");

Return the result
return result;
}
```

Publishing our CDS response

So far, we have published a CDS request message, used our quant library to price the CDS, and published the response. The only thing left to do is to let the world know our results, like this:

```
public bool ProcessCDSResponse(CreditDefaultSwapResponseMessage cds)
{
Console.WriteLine("calculated spread: " + cds.fairRate);
Console.WriteLine("calculated NPV: " + cds.fairNPV);
return true;
}
```

Calculating a CDS

With all the mechanics of message-publishing and subscribing out of the way, let's talk about the actual CDS calculation. Our quant library does an excellent job of abstracting the many details away from us when it comes to quantitative finance. All we have to do is decide what we want and call the proper functions. This makes our microservice very business-specific, which is one of our key objectives. Since this is not a book on quantitative finance, I will not delve into the details of what is happening here; the important message is that you don't care. To you, it's a white or black box, the same as any other third-party toolkit that you use. Sometimes you have the source and know what's going on under the hood (in this case you do), and sometimes you don't.

The following is the code for calculating a CDS:

```
public bool CalcCDS(ref CreditDefaultSwapRequestMessage msg, double
fixedRate, double notional, double recoveryRate)
{
// Testing fair-spread calculation for credit-default swaps...
using (SavedSettings backup = new SavedSettings())
{
```

```
// Initialize curves
Calendar calendar = new TARGET();
Date today = calendar.adjust(Date.Today);
Settings.setEvaluationDate(today);
Handle<Quote> hazardRate = new Handle<Quote>(new SimpleQuote(0.01234));
RelinkableHandle<DefaultProbabilityTermStructure> probabilityCurve = new
RelinkableHandle<DefaultProbabilityTermStructure>();
probabilityCurve.linkTo(new FlatHazardRate(0, calendar, hazardRate, new
Actual360()));
RelinkableHandle<YieldTermStructure> discountCurve =
new RelinkableHandle<YieldTermStructure>();
discountCurve.linkTo(new FlatForward(today, 0.06, new Actual360()));
// Build the schedule
Date issueDate = calendar.advance(today, -1, TimeUnit.Years);
Date maturity = calendar.advance(issueDate, 10, TimeUnit.Years);
BusinessDayConvention convention = BusinessDayConvention.Following;
Schedule schedule = new MakeSchedule().from(issueDate)
.to(maturity)
.withFrequency(Frequency.Quarterly)
.withCalendar(calendar)
.withTerminationDateConvention(convention)
.withRule(DateGeneration.Rule.TwentiethIMM).value();
// Build the CDS
DayCounter dayCount = new Actual360();
IPricingEngine engine = new MidPointCdsEngine(probabilityCurve,
recoveryRate, discountCurve);
CreditDefaultSwap cds = new CreditDefaultSwap(Protection.Side.Seller,
notional, fixedRate,
schedule, convention, dayCount, true, true);
cds.setPricingEngine(engine);
double fairRate = cds.fairSpread();
CreditDefaultSwap fairCds = new CreditDefaultSwap(Protection.Side.Seller,
notional, fairRate,
schedule, convention, dayCount, true, true);
fairCds.setPricingEngine(engine);
double fairNPV = fairCds.NPV();
double tolerance = 1e-10;
msg.fairRate = fairRate;
msg.fairNPV = fairNPV;
return (Math.Abs(fairNPV) <= tolerance);
}
```

Getting bond information

Now let's skim over how we do exactly the same thing with our bonds. First, let's take a brief look at the request message itself. As was the case with the CDSs, the response message is a mirror of this one so we won't show it:

```
/// <summary> (Serializable) the bonds request message. </summary>
[Queue("Financial", ExchangeName = "EvolvedAI")]
[Serializable]
public class BondsRequestMessage
{
public DateTime issue { get; set; }
public DateTime maturity { get; set; }
public double coupon { get; set; }
public int frequency { get; set; }
public double yield { get; set; }
public string compounding { get; set; }\
public double price { get; set; }
public double calcYield { get; set; }
public double price2 { get; set; }
public string message { get; set; }
}
```

Processing a bond request

When we receive a request for bond information, our message processor is much simpler than it was for our CDS. Once someone posts a message to the effect that they need bond info, we receive `BondRequestMessage` with the information we need filled in. From there, we calculate the remaining information, as shown here. Again, this is a black box by design, so we don't concern ourselves with the technicalities underlying how a bond; is a bond, we let our quant library do what it does best:

```
public bool ProcessBondsMessage(BondsRequestMessage msg)
{
Bonds b = new Bonds();
return b.testYield(this);
}
```

Processing a bond response

Once we have received a request for bond information, calculated all the bond information, and posted the response, someone will be listening for the results. They do that by subscribing to BondsResponseMessage as follows. As soon as they do this, they will only be receiving the responses, which means we are only interested in the final results. Once we receive this message, we can post the details of the bond, perform another step in our workflow, and so forth:

```
public bool ProcessBondsResponse(BondsResponseMessage msg)
{
Console.WriteLine(msg.message + ":n"
+ " issue: " + msg.issue + "n"
+ " maturity: " + msg.maturity + "n"
+ " coupon: " + msg.coupon + "n"
+ " frequency: " + msg.frequency + "nn"
+ " yield: " + msg.yield + " "
+ msg.compounding + "n"
+ " price: " + msg.price + "n"
+ " yield': " + msg.calcYield + "n"
+ " price': " + msg.price2};
return true;
}
```

This is what our application looks like while it is running. It has processed one CDS and one bond:

```
QuantFinanceMicroService                                           —   □   ×
    issue:      5/22/2020 12:00:00 AM
    maturity:   5/22/2040 12:00:00 AM
    coupon:     0.08
    frequency: 1

    yield:  0.05 continuous
    price:  135.412004023351
    yield': 0.05
    price': 135.412004023351
yield recalculation failed::
    issue:      5/22/2020 12:00:00 AM
    maturity:   5/22/2040 12:00:00 AM
    coupon:     0.08
    frequency: 1

    yield:  0.06 continuous
    price:  120.517567649524
    yield': 0.0600000381469727
    price': 120.517515175551
yield recalculation failed::
    issue:      5/22/2020 12:00:00 AM
    maturity:   5/22/2040 12:00:00 AM
    coupon:     0.08
    frequency: 1

    yield:  0.07 continuous
    price:  107.775023706766
    yield': 0.0699999622344971
    price': 107.775068219188
```

Summary

In this chapter, we exposed you to the world of qualitative finance and the great open source package, QLNet. We used this package to distribute information about bonds and CDSs. We sent and received messages to show you a complete messaging loop. All you need to do now is continue to follow this paradigm and modify things to suit your needs.

Exercises

1. Price your financial instruments however you normally do
2. Do not publish the request message in the constructor or `OnStart` method
3. Find a more suitable way to publish the request

11
Trello Microservice – Board Status Updating

This chapter introduces a microservice that every corporate American entity can use: the **Trello microservice**. It is designed to work with Trello, which is a collaboration tool. For those familiar with JIRA and TFS, it's the same Kanban board approach, with an arguably simpler and more intuitive user interface. Just picture a wall in your office filled with sticky notes of to-do items, tasks, notes, pictures, and so on. Now, organize that into a simple and intuitive user interface and you have Trello.

You can become more familiar with Trello by visiting their website at `https://trello.com/tour`.

In this chapter, we will learn about the following:

- How to use the Trello application programming interface
- How to develop a microservice that talks to Trello

Installation

Before we do anything, we need to create a free account on Trello so that you can see the boards, cards, and lists that have been created. Alternatively, you can install the Windows 10 Trello application if applicable. If you are having trouble generating cards with the microservice as is, please go to `https://trello.com/app-key` and generate your own key. Once you have done that, simply replace the key with your newly generated one in the following call in the `OnStart` method:

```
trello = new Trello("9dbf8c09499d07abac02bbd6d5af4b9c");
```

Replace the token you get with the one in this call (the same method):

```
trello.Authorize("95da70bf03bd43b82648f515477d44ec84baa2fb9e811cb7284be10d9
4512b81");
```

Next, let's go ahead and create another **Console App (.NET Framework)** for our microservice. We will name this one `TrelloMicroService`:

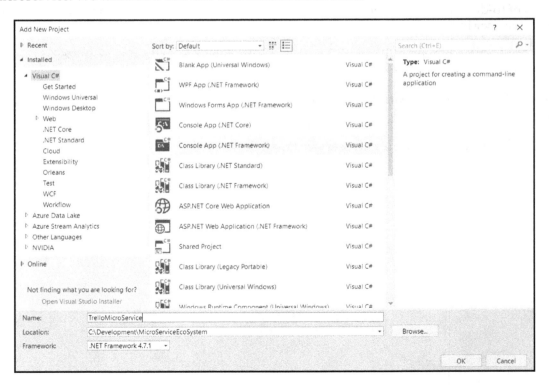

For this microservice, we will be using an open source package, `TrelloNet`, which makes working with Trello and its REST API very simple. In fact, it makes it perfect for programmatic implementation within a microservice. Imagine you receive an email with specific words in it, and from that you automatically create a ticket, assign it, and give it a due date. Based upon a reaction to a specific event, you could then automatically close out tickets and boards if you so desired.

Let's install our `TrelloNet` NuGet package, as shown in the following screenshot:

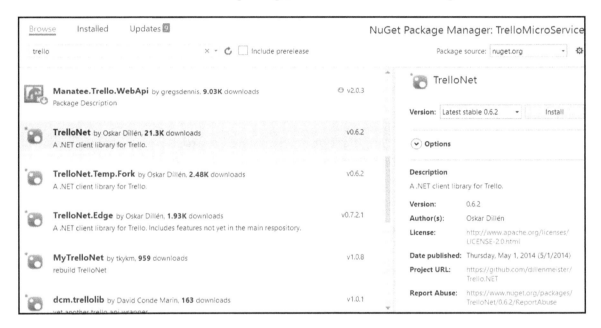

Creating boards, lists, and cards

The following code shows how we will create a board, three chapter lists, and then add 10 chapters per list with due dates, all in just a few lines of code:

```
var expectedBoard = CreateBoard("Microservice Ecosystem", "Hands on
Microservices with C#");
var expectedList = CreateList("Drafts");
for (int x=0; x<10; x++)
CreateCard("Chapter " + (x + 1).ToString(), RandomString(25), false,
x % 2 == 0
?
SystemClock.Instance.GetCurrentInstant().ToDateTimeUtc().ToLocalTime().AddD
```

```
ays(12)
: DateTime.MinValue);
CreateList("Proofs");
for (int x = 0; x < 10; x++)
CreateCard("Chapter " + (x + 1).ToString(), RandomString(25), false,
x % 2 == 0
?
SystemClock.Instance.GetCurrentInstant().ToDateTimeUtc().ToLocalTime().AddD
ays(24)
: DateTime.MinValue);
CreateList("Final Copies");
for (int x = 0; x < 10; x++)
CreateCard("Chapter " + (x + 1).ToString(), RandomString(25), false,
x % 2 == 0
?
SystemClock.Instance.GetCurrentInstant().ToDateTimeUtc().ToLocalTime().AddD
ays(36)
: DateTime.MinValue);
```

After the previous calls, we will see that our newly created board, Microservice Ecosystem, has appeared on the board list. The command that did this was:

```
var expectedBoard = CreateBoard("Microservice Ecosystem", "Hands on
Microservices with C#");
```

Once our board is created you can open Trello and see it displayed along with your other boards:

If we open our board, we can see that we have three lists that we created; **Drafts**,
Proofs, and **Final Copies**. In each list, we have 10 chapters that we added. Every other
chapter has a due date:

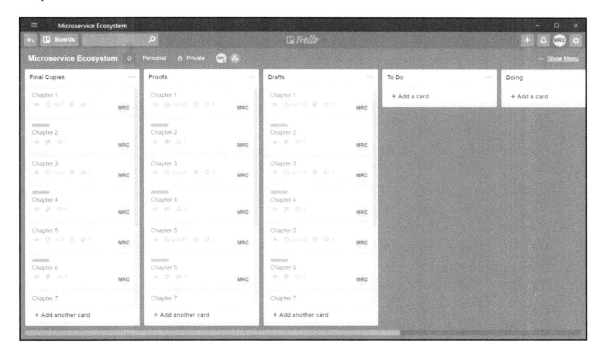

If you click on any of the chapters and open it up, you will see a detailed view similar to what you see in the following screenshot. In this example, you can see that we set an automatic **Due Date** of **tomorrow at 5:03 AM (due soon)**:

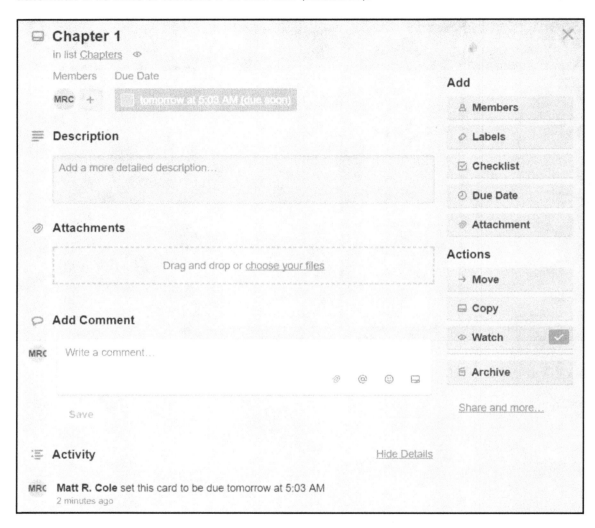

Here is another view of our chapter card, showing how you could easily customize several more properties if you so desired:

With that done, we are going to close this chapter a bit differently. We are going to leave the remaining implementation of this microservice to you, the reader. Sort of a weird pop quiz, if you will. Just complete the `TrelloRequestMessage`, send the messages, subscribe to the messages, and process accordingly.

Summary

In this chapter, we introduced you to Trello and how we can create a microservice in order to programmatically create tickets (boards, cards, and lists) for our product. We also took a wide turn in that we showed you how to use the NuGet package to make events happen, but have left the final implementation up to you.

In the next chapter we will develop our Microservice manager, nicknamed the 'Nexus', to control all our microservices.

Exercises

Here are some exercises for your consideration:

1. Complete the `TrelloRequestMessage` so that your microservice can create Trello items via messages
2. Create a board specific for you
3. Customize each list and card to meet your needs

Microservice Manager – The Nexus 12

The microservice manager is, by some aspects, next to RabbitMQ, the heart or nexus of the system. It is the main brain, if you will, of the ecosystem. From it, we can control different aspects of the system as well as send and receive messages. You can have it do anything that you like, it's your blank canvas. In our world, we wanted to subscribe to all our messages, and once they were received, display them to the user. You, of course, will do different things once you make the code production ready for your world. But the microservice manager can trigger events, listen for events, and trigger more events predicated upon responses; it's really whatever you can dream up.

In this chapter we will cover:

1. Developing a centralized Microservice Manager
2. Integrating all previous message subscriptions
3. Process all previously received messages

As we said, in our world, just to give you some idea, our microservice manager will be subscribing to all the messages we are sending. Where there are two messages, one for request and one for response, we will be subscribing to the response message. You could very easily expand this to listen for the request messages and then keep track of who does and does not send our responses. It could be a good first indicator of a microservice degrading in its service capabilities! You could also use the cache manager to track the number/volume of each request and issue a report on this at a predetermined time.

The health status messages are probably the most important. If you log these into a database, you will have a temporal history of your entire ecosystem, and again, you can use that information to generate reports as needed. Day one of your microservices doesn't calculate a **Credit Default Swap** (**CDS**), price a bond, or something else critical to the business needs; trust me when I say you'll be very glad you have this information as a reference.

Installation

Our first task is to create our console application, as we have done with every microservice. We will do so as shown in the following figure:

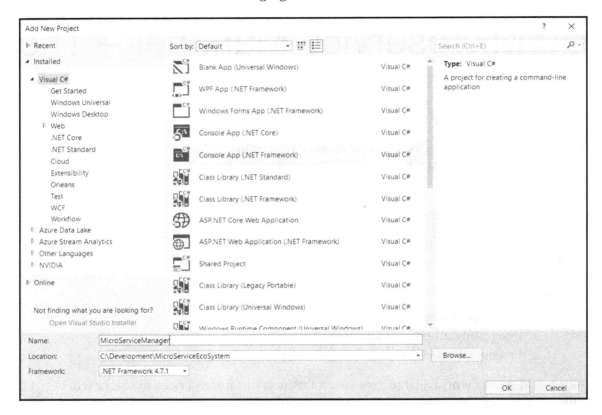

Once the project is created, we need to install our NuGet packages for use. In this case, we are going to install and use a great open source package that is perhaps one of the most useful and easiest caching mechanisms I've used, `CacheManager`. This product will help us to store information when and where we need it, and has numerous types of runtime processing:

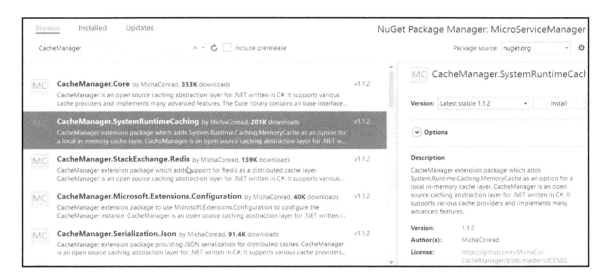

Installing `Topshelf.Leader`:

Our code

Before we get started, we should look at the biggest and baddest `main.cs` we've done so far. Nothing but the best for our manager, right? Refer to the following code to see what we have done:

```
static void Main(string[] args)
{
var builder = new ContainerBuilder();
// Service itself
builder.RegisterType<MSBaseLogger>()?.SingleInstance();
builder.RegisterType<MicroServiceManager>()
.AsImplementedInterfaces()
.AsSelf()
?.InstancePerLifetimeScope();
//builder.AttachInterceptorsToRegistrations(new
LogInterceptor(Console.Out));
_container = builder.Build();
XmlConfigurator.ConfigureAndWatch(new FileInfo(@".log4net.config"));
HostFactory.Run(c =>
{
c?.UseAutofacContainer(_container);
c?.UseLog4Net();
c?.ApplyCommandLineWithDebuggerSupport();
c?.EnablePauseAndContinue();
c?.EnableShutdown();
c?.OnException(ex => Console.WriteLine(ex.Message));
c?.UseWindowsHostEnvironmentWithDebugSupport();
c?.Service<MicroServiceManager>(s =>
{
s.ConstructUsingAutofacContainer<MicroServiceManager>();
s?.ConstructUsing(settings =>
{
var service =
AutofacHostBuilderConfigurator.LifetimeScope.Resolve<MicroServiceManager>()
;
return service;
});
s?.ConstructUsing(name => new MicroServiceManager(_container,
Guid.NewGuid().ToString()));
s?.WhenStartedAsLeader(b =>
{
b.WhenStarted(async (service, token) =>
{
await service.Start(token);
});
b.Lease(lcb => lcb.RenewLeaseEvery(TimeSpan.FromSeconds(2))
```

```
.AquireLeaseEvery(TimeSpan.FromSeconds(5))
.LeaseLength(TimeSpan.FromDays(1))
.WithLeaseManager(new MicroServiceManager()));
b.WithHeartBeat(TimeSpan.FromSeconds(30), (isLeader, token) =>
Task.CompletedTask);
b.Build();
});
s?.WhenStarted((MicroServiceManager server, HostControl host) =>
server.OnStart(host));
s?.WhenPaused(server => server?.OnPause());
s?.WhenContinued(server => server?.OnResume());
s?.WhenStopped(server => server?.OnStop());
s?.WhenShutdown(server => server?.OnShutdown());
s?.WhenCustomCommandReceived((server, host, code) => { });
s?.AfterStartingService(() => { });
s?.AfterStoppingService(() => { });
s?.BeforeStartingService(() => { });
s?.BeforeStoppingService(() => { });
});
c?.RunAsNetworkService();
c?.StartAutomaticallyDelayed();
c?.SetDescription(string.Intern("MicroService Manager Sample"));
c?.SetDisplayName(string.Intern("MicroServiceManager"));
c?.SetServiceName(string.Intern("MicroServiceManager"));
c?.EnableServiceRecovery(r =>
{
r?.OnCrashOnly();
r?.RestartService(1); //first
r?.RestartService(1); //second
r?.RestartService(1); //subsequents
r?.SetResetPeriod(0);
});
});
}
```

Leader election

In this instance, we are using the `WhenStartedAsLeader()` method from a wonderful third-party extension titled `Topshelf.Leader`, which we installed via our NuGet package mechanism, the same as we have done before. This provides us with something known in computer science as **leader election**. Leader election is the process by which a single process can be designated as the leader among several distributed processes. In the beginning, no process knows who the leader is. They must agree on which one will assume this role. That is exactly the functionality that the `Topshelf.Leader` framework provides. It accomplishes the purpose of consensus management. Rather than write about consensus management (which could take a book by itself), I will refer you to Wikipedia and start you off with the Paxos algorithm: `https://en.wikipedia.org/wiki/Paxos_(computer_science)`.

Moving on, our `main.cs` file now uses the `WhenStartedAsLeader()` extension method, which contains its own version of the `WhenStarted()` method, one with cancellation-token support. Because we want one Bitcoin microservice controlling many if needed, and because we want them to handle leadership among themselves (who will take the next message, and so on), it is important that we have this leadership determination capability.

The `WhenStarted()` method will be executed when the service discovers that it is the current leader. If that situation changes, the cancellation token will be set to cancelled. We will leave it up to the aspiring developer to enhance this method to do whatever you think is appropriate for your scenario.

We should mention that the Bitcoin microservice implements the `ILeaseManager` interface, which means that the responsibility for deciding on the leader falls with the microservice. Our microservice will call the `AcquireLease()` function until it gets a lease, meaning we are the leader. Once that happens, we run the `WhenStarted` delegate as instructed.

While all this is happening, we are still renewing our lease every few seconds. We stop the service and release the lease back to the next potential leader.

Subscribing to all messages

Being the center of our ecosystem, our microservice will be subscribing to all messages. So let's now take a look at what our `Subscribe` method looks like, in all its glory. You will notice that we first declare our `exchange` and then our `queue`, just in case they do not exist for some reason. After that, we bind each `queue` to an `exchange`. Finally, we subscribe to all our messages, and provide our handlers for the processing of each message, as shown in the highlighted code:

```
public void Subscribe()
{
Bus = RabbitHutch.CreateBus("host=localhost");
IExchange exchange = Bus.Advanced.ExchangeDeclare("EvolvedAI",
ExchangeType.Topic);
IQueue queue = Bus.Advanced.QueueDeclare("HealthStatus");
Bus.Advanced.Bind(exchange, queue, "");
queue = Bus.Advanced.QueueDeclare("Memory");
Bus.Advanced.Bind(exchange, queue, "");
queue = Bus.Advanced.QueueDeclare("Deployments");
Bus.Advanced.Bind(exchange, queue, "");
queue = Bus.Advanced.QueueDeclare("FileSystem");
Bus.Advanced.Bind(exchange, queue, "");
Bus.Subscribe<HealthStatusMessage>("", msg => {
ProcessHealthMessage(msg); },
config => config?.WithTopic("HealthStatus"));
Bus.Subscribe<MemoryUpdateMessage>("", msg => {
ProcessMemoryMessage(msg); },
config => config?.WithTopic("MemoryStatus"));
Bus.Subscribe<DeploymentStartMessage>("", msg => {
ProcessDeploymentStartMessage(msg); },
config => config?.WithTopic("Deployments.Start"));
Bus.Subscribe<DeploymentStopMessage>("", msg => {
ProcessDeploymentStopMessage(msg); },
config => config?.WithTopic("Deployments.Stop"));
Bus.Subscribe<FileSystemChangeMessage>("", msg => {
ProcessFileSystemMessage(msg); },
config => config?.WithTopic("FileSystemChanges"));
Bus.Subscribe<CreditDefaultSwapResponseMessage>("", msg => {
ProcessCDSMessage(msg); },
config => config?.WithTopic("CDSResponse"));
Bus.Subscribe<BondsResponseMessage>("", msg => {
ProcessBondMessage(msg); },
config => config?.WithTopic("BondResponse"));
Bus?.Subscribe<MLMessage>(Environment.MachineName, msg =>
ProcessMachineLearningMessage(msg),
config => config?.WithTopic("MachineLearning"));
```

```
Bus?.Subscribe<BitcoinSpendReceipt>(Environment.MachineName, msg =>
ProcessBitcoinSpendReceiptMessage(msg),
config => config?.WithTopic("Bitcoin"));
}
```

What do our handlers look like? Since this is our manager, let's discuss each one.

 Whether or not you decide to act on any message is up to you, but whatever decision you make, someone is always going to ask the question, *Who's watching the watcher?* This simply means that if there's one center piece to your puzzle, we must make sure that it is running and performing as desired. Otherwise, we have a single bottleneck and that's no good. You can accomplish this by making sure that the microservice-manager process is being watched by whatever corporate tools you have available for monitoring applications or processes, **Orion** is commonly found in corporate America. This way, if it goes down, an alert is triggered and you can take the appropriate action.

Processing bond response messages

This message is generated in response to `BondsRequestMessage`, where someone is theoretically asking to price a bond. In our examples, everything is theoretical, but there's no reason you can't hook it up to a Bloomberg service license and get the information in real time. Regardless of how you do it, this shows the process of request-response and how to do it. As a microservice manager, we don't care about the work going on, as long as it goes on. What we do care about are the completions and results, which, in production, we would store or report upon:

```
bool ProcessBondMessage([NotNull] BondsResponseMessage msg)
{
Console.WriteLine("Received Bonds Response Message");
RILogManager.Default?.SendInformation("Received Bonds Response Message");
Console.WriteLine(msg.message + ":n"
+ " issue: " + msg.issue + "n"
+ " maturity: " + msg.maturity + "n"
+ " coupon: " + msg.coupon + "n"
+ " frequency: " + msg.frequency + "nn"
+ " yield: " + msg.yield + " "
+ msg.compounding + "n"
+ " price: " + msg.price + "n"
+ " yield': " + msg.calcYield + "n"
+ " price': " + msg.price2);
return true;
}
```

Processing deployment messages

There are two deployment messages—a start and a stop. The start is generated at the start of a software deployment, and the stop is generated at its completion. In between, we track the time and, if 15 minutes elapses from the start without receiving a stop message, we will trigger an alert that the deployment is taking too long and should be checked:

```
bool ProcessDeploymentStartMessage([NotNull] DeploymentStartMessage msg)
{
Console.WriteLine("Received DeploymentStart Message");
RILogManager.Default?.SendInformation("Received DeploymentStart Message");
return true;
}
bool ProcessDeploymentStopMessage([NotNull] DeploymentStopMessage msg)
{
Console.WriteLine("Received DeploymentStop Message");
RILogManager.Default?.SendInformation("Received DeploymentStop Message");
return true;
}
```

Processing CDS messages

This function shows you how we are processing a response for a CDS. Once the CDS has been processed, depending upon the result, you could choose from a myriad of different avenues. For instance, once complete, you may decide to process another CDS or bond, or send an email. Think about the individual actions that you would take and we could probably turn them into messages and microservices:

```
bool ProcessCDSMessage([NotNull] CreditDefaultSwapResponseMessage msg)
{
Console.WriteLine("Received Credit Default Swap Response Message");
RILogManager.Default?.SendInformation("Received Credit Default Swap Response Message");
Console.WriteLine("calculated spread: " + msg.fairRate);
Console.WriteLine("calculated NPV: " + msg.fairNPV);
return true;
}
```

Processing memory messages

Our memory microservice is responsible for tracking the memory consumption of our apps as well as triggering the garbage collector to free up memory. It will also report the status of that effort. It's up to you as to how you want to enhance the memory microservice to meet your needs; there are countless ways you could do so. But for now, we simply want to acknowledge that we received the message:

```
bool ProcessMemoryMessage([NotNull] MemoryUpdateMessage msg)
{
Console.WriteLine("Received Memory Update Message");
RILogManager.Default?.SendInformation("Received Memory Update Message");
return true;
}
```

Processing health status messages

Each microservice will send a health status message to let us know it's alright and working properly. As the microservice manager, it's our responsibility to track this, log the information, and trigger alerts if necessary. The health status message will also send us the amount of memory it is using as well as the CPU usage:

```
bool ProcessHealthMessage([NotNull] HealthStatusMessage msg)
{
Console.WriteLine("Received Health Status Message");
RILogManager.Default?.SendInformation("Received Health Status Message");
RILogManager.Default?.SendInformation(msg.serviceName);
RILogManager.Default?.SendInformation(msg.status.ToString());
RILogManager.Default?.SendInformation(ToBytes(msg.memoryUsed));
RILogManager.Default?.SendInformation(msg.CPU.ToString());
RILogManager.Default?.SendInformation(msg.message);
Console.WriteLine(msg.serviceName);
Console.WriteLine(msg.status.ToString());
Console.WriteLine(ToBytes(msg.memoryUsed));
Console.WriteLine(msg.CPU.ToString());
Console.WriteLine(msg.message);
return true;
}
```

Processing machine learning messages

The machine learning response message will be generated once a machine learning effort has taken place. We only care about the responses, not the ground level work that goes on prior to learning completion:

```
bool ProcessMachineLearningMessage(MLMessage msg)
{
Console.WriteLine("Received Machine Learning Response Message");
RILogManager.Default?.SendInformation("Received Machine Learning Response
Message");
return true;
}
```

Processing filesystem messages

The `FileSystemChangeMessage` will alert us when a filesystem event has taken place. Examples of such would be files being FTP'd into a directory for us, files being deleted and created, and folders being renamed. The most realistic example I can provide is us monitoring a directory for files to arrive, and once they do, triggering our ETL jobs to load the data:

```
bool ProcessFileSystemMessage([NotNull] FileSystemChangeMessage msg)
{
Console.WriteLine("Received FileSystemChange Message");
RILogManager.Default?.SendInformation("Received FileSystemChange Message");
Console.WriteLine("*********************");
Console.WriteLine("Changed Date = {0}", msg.ChangeDate);
Console.WriteLine("ChangeType = {0}", msg.ChangeType);
Console.WriteLine("FullPath = {0}", msg.FullPath);
Console.WriteLine("OldPath = {0}", msg.OldPath);
Console.WriteLine("Name = {0}", msg.Name);
Console.WriteLine("Old Name = {0}", msg.OldName);
Console.WriteLine("FileSystemEventType {0}", (int)msg.EventType);
Console.WriteLine("*********************");
// This is our new highlighted section
using (var database = new LiteDatabase(connectionString))
{
database.Shrink();
var collection = database.GetCollection<FileSystemChangeMessage>();
collection.EnsureIndex(x => x.ID);
collection.Insert(msg);
}
return true;
}
```

If you notice the highlighted section previously, this is actually in every processing function, but for brevity I chose not to show it until here. It writes out whatever record we have to our document database (**LiteDB**) according to message type. We simply connect to our database, reduce the occupied space of the database, find the message type we are interested in, ensure it has an index, and then insert the record.

Summary

In this chapter, we learned how to build a filesystem watcher and contain it within a microservice that we can start and stop as desired. Messages are both printed to the console and obtained by the microservice manager to keep track of.

Exercises

Here are a few exercises you can choose to do on your own.

1. Optimize how messages are subscribed to and handled
2. Run multiple instances and ensure the leadership mechanism is properly instrumented for your situation
3. Implement power handling (battery low, unplugged, and so on)
4. Complete LiteDB document storage for your situation (the highlighted sections that are in all processing functions)

13
Creating a Blockchain Bitcoin Microservice

Blockchain, Bitcoin, you hear that as much as you hear the terms big data and **artificial intelligence** (**AI**) thrown around. What is blockchain technology, you might ask? I've heard of Bitcoin but never used it, and what does that have to do with a microservice? Well, the same way I showed you how to turn a machine learning and quant financial framework into a microservice, so shall we do here.

In this chapter we will cover:

1. Blockchain and Bitcoin theory
2. Building a Bitcoin microservice
3. Show you how you can spend digital cash

Blockchain

According to Don and Alex Tapscott, authors of *Blockchain Revolution* (2016),

> *"The blockchain is an incorruptible digital ledger of economic transactions that can be programmed to record not just financial transactions but virtually everything of value."*

The blockchain is the database of all transactions that have happened since the beginning of time. In the blockchain world, this is known as the **genesis block**. The blockchain is duplicated all over the world. Once a transaction of something appears in the blockchain, it is very easy to prove it exists.

In this world, miners are entities whose only goal in life is to insert a transaction into the blockchain. To be efficient, miners try to update batches of transactions into a **block**. Other nodes confirm that this new block obeys all rules set forth in the Bitcoin protocol. Once a miner inserts an update into the blockchain, all transactions inside that block are considered confirmed. At this point, you have a row in a database that can never be erased.

That means basically that blockchain technology, originally created for Bitcoin, can really be used for any kind of transaction, and the digital-technology community is catching on to that fast. A blockchain can be thought of as a decentralized database that is managed by distributed computers on a peer-to-peer network. Each peer maintains a copy of the ledge to prevent a single point of failure. Updates and copying are reflected across all peers simultaneously.

Bitcoin

Bitcoin itself, in a nutshell, is either virtual currency or referencing the technology, depending upon who you talk to. Some very interesting things happen with a Bitcoin transaction:

- It is irreversible, period.
- It is pseudonymous. Nothing is related to any real-world identity.
- It's fast and global. Transactions are confirmed in just a few minutes, regardless of physical location.
- It's secure. Since Bitcoin money is locked in a cryptography system, only the owner of the private key can send currency.
- You need no permissions.

If you are not familiar with this technology, and perhaps actually do live under that proverbial rock, let me explain why you should not worry too much about the safety of your money. Just remember, it's virtual, so could something go wrong, sure. But think about this.

You go into a store to make a purchase. You use your credit card to pay. There's no signature on the back. You sign the receipt. You walk out with your purchase. Did that make you feel safe? How much effort did the cashier really put into verifying that it's you? But you don't worry, because you have *nobody-paid-attention* insurance from your major credit card. You can dispute it any time. But wasn't that all virtual as well? You just trusted someone you've never met with your finances.

The blockchain, and Bitcoin, use a peer-to-peer decentralized system to conduct transactions. They employ asymmetric cryptography using elliptical curves to make transactions secure, and one of the keys is **digital signatures**.

Digital signatures

This is perhaps the most important tool used in cryptocurrency. A signature is, you, right? But how will we, just as we do with that physical paper signature, verify you as you? We start with four very basic assumptions:

- Our digital signature needs to verify you are you and do it with 100% accuracy every time
- It should be non-forgeable and non-copyable
- Non-repudiation, meaning if you signed it, you own it, and it was you and no one else but you
- Your signature is your public and private key

The circle of encryption

Everything within the circle of encryption requires your private key. You and only you have it, remember? You didn't give it to your partner for safekeeping, the nanny for emergencies, you kept it safe and stored it away where only you can access it. If you followed that simple, easy step, then welcome to the circle of encryption:

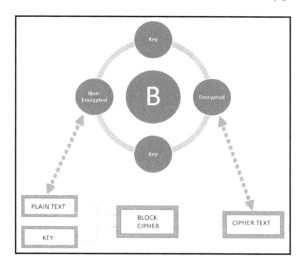

How does the text get encrypted? By taking the **PLAIN TEXT**, combining that with the private **KEY**, and creating what is called a **BLOCK CIPHER**. You now have an encrypted **CIPHER TEXT**:

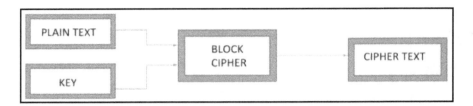

And, of course, we apply the reverse to decrypt the encrypted text. We have to have the private key in order to do this. Remember, given the private key, anyone can decipher the data from encrypted data and vice versa. Now, if you are dealing with just plain strings, I'd be worried. But we are dealing with huge chunks of structured data, which makes it a nearly insurmountable task to crack your encryption.

There are two rules for a block cipher to be considered valid:

- We must be able to derive the plain text from the cipher key and vice versa given a key
- The function must be efficiently computable

Installation

In this microservice, we are going to leverage the awesome NBitcoin and QBitNinja.Client open source packages. We will install them via NuGet packages, just like every other microservice. Here are what the NuGet packages look like:

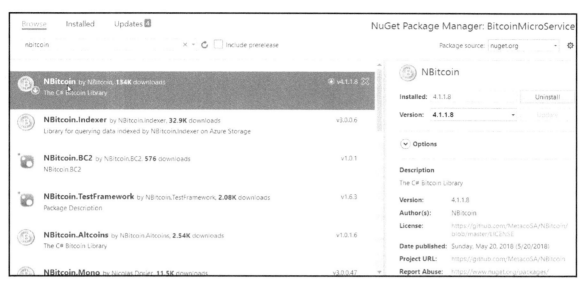

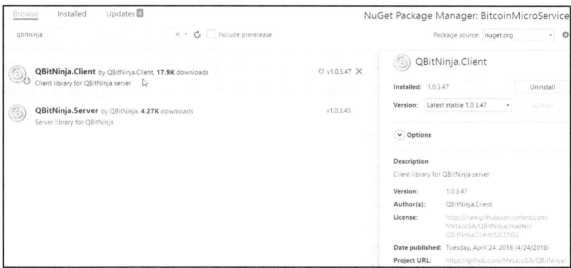

Our main program

Here's our `main.cs`, and you will notice that it differs from what we've seen before. The different sections are highlighted as follows:

```
static void Main(string[] args)
{
var builder = new ContainerBuilder();
// Service itself
builder.RegisterType<MSBaseLogger>()?.SingleInstance();
builder.RegisterType<BitcoinMS>()
.AsImplementedInterfaces()
.AsSelf()
?.InstancePerLifetimeScope();
_container = builder.Build();
XmlConfigurator.ConfigureAndWatch(new FileInfo(@".log4net.config"));
HostFactory.Run(c =>
{
c?.UseAutofacContainer(_container);
c?.UseLog4Net();
c?.ApplyCommandLineWithDebuggerSupport();
c?.EnablePauseAndContinue();
c?.EnableShutdown();
c?.OnException(ex => Console.WriteLine(ex.Message));
c?.Service<BitcoinMS>(s =>
{
s.ConstructUsingAutofacContainer<BitcoinMS>();
s?.ConstructUsing(settings =>
{
var service =
AutofacHostBuilderConfigurator.LifetimeScope.Resolve<BitcoinMS>();
return service;
});
s?.ConstructUsing(name => new BitcoinMS(_container, new
Guid().ToString()));

// Here is where our code is different
s.WhenStartedAsLeader(b =>
{
b.WhenStarted(async (service, token) =>
{
await service.Start(token);
});
b.Lease(lcb => lcb.RenewLeaseEvery(TimeSpan.FromSeconds(2))
.AquireLeaseEvery(TimeSpan.FromSeconds(5))
.LeaseLength(TimeSpan.FromDays(1))
.WithLeaseManager(new BitcoinMS())));
```

```
b.WithHeartBeat(TimeSpan.FromSeconds(30), (isLeader, token) =>
Task.CompletedTask);
});


s?.WhenPaused(server => server?.OnPause());
s?.WhenContinued(server => server?.OnResume());
s?.WhenStopped(server => server?.OnStop());
s?.WhenShutdown(server => server?.OnShutdown());
});
c?.RunAsNetworkService();
c?.StartAutomaticallyDelayed();
c?.SetDescription(string.Intern("Bitcoin Manager Sample"));
c?.SetDisplayName(string.Intern("BitcoinMicroService"));
c?.SetServiceName(string.Intern("BitcoinMicroService"));
c?.EnableServiceRecovery(r =>
{
r?.OnCrashOnly();
r?.RestartService(1); //first
r?.RestartService(1); //second
r?.RestartService(1); //subsequents
r?.SetResetPeriod(0);
});
});
}
```

Leader election

In this instance, we are using the `WhenStartedAsLeader` method from a wonderful third-party extension entitled `Topshelf.Leader`, which we installed via our `NuGet` package mechanism, the same as we have done before. This provides us with something known in computer science as leader election. Leader election is the process by which a single process can be designated as the leader among several distributed processes. In the beginning, no process knows who the leader is. They must agree on which one will assume this role. That is exactly the functionality the `Topshelf.Leader` framework provides.

We now use the `WhenStartedAsLeader()` extension method, which contains its own version of the `WhenStarted()` method, one with cancellation-token support. We want one Bitcoin microservice controlling many if needed, and we want them to handle leadership among themselves (who will take the next message, and so on).

The `WhenStarted()` method will be executed when the service discovers that it is the current leader. If that situation changes, the cancellation token will be set to cancelled. We will leave it up to the aspiring developer to enhance this method to do whatever you think is appropriate for your scenario.

We should mention that the Bitcoin microservice implements the `ILeaseManager` interface, which means that the responsibility for deciding on the leader falls to the microservice. Our microservice will call the `AcquireLease()` function until it gets a lease, meaning we are the leader. Once that happens, we run the `WhenStarted` delegate as instructed.

While all this is happening, we are still renewing our lease every few seconds. When we stop the service, we release the lease back to the next potential leader.

Creating our digital wallet

To be technically accurate, Bitcoins are not stored anywhere physically, such as inside a bank vault; there is a private key (secret number) for every Bitcoin address that is saved in the Bitcoin wallet of the person who owns the balance. Bitcoin wallets facilitate sending and receiving Bitcoins and give ownership of the Bitcoin balance to the user. Just as Bitcoins are the digital equivalent of cash, a Bitcoin wallet is analogous to a physical wallet.

There are four different kinds of wallets:

- **Desktop**: These are installed on a desktop computer.
- **Mobile**: These are located on your mobile devices for easier access. These also allow for *touch-to-pay* applications using **Near-Field Communications** (**NFC**) or a QR code to scan.
- **Web**: Web combines mobile and browsers.
- **Hardware**: The most secure form of a Bitcoin wallet. They are stored on a physical equipment item, such as a flash drive via a USB port.

Before we create our wallet, we need to generate our public key. There is a great website, `WalletGenerator.Net`, that will make it fun and exciting to do so. I would recommend following the process of moving your mouse around to generate more randomness in the new public address and watch the data being generated:

Our **Public Address** comes from our private key, and the following diagram shows you various pieces of information, including the **Wallet-Interchange Format (WIF)**:

Your public address

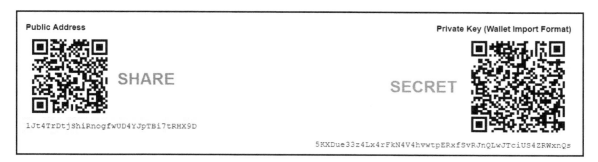

What, a **Public Address**? How do I know that is secure? Well, in order to get that seemingly easily-hackable **Public Address**, the mathematicians behind the scenes have done the following:

- Parse the **Private Key** through an SHA 256 hashing algorithm
- With that hash, parse it through the RIPE MD 160 function and a new hash will be generated (a copy will be made)
- Send that hash code through the SHA 256 algorithm to generate another hash
- Send that hash code back through the SHA 256 algorithm and save the first 7 bits
- Take the hash from the RIPE MD 160 and add it to the last hash code we just received, and we have a **Public Address**

That should help you see just how secure the system is designed to be.

How do we spend money?

Since I'm not allowed to give investment advice, nor would I ever, I recommend checking out the many good online sources for all information regarding blockchain and Bitcoin. Start with `https://bitcoin.org/en/`:

Introduction   Resources   Innovation   Participate   FAQ   English

Getting started with Bitcoin

Using Bitcoin to pay and get paid is easy and accessible to everyone.

How to use Bitcoin

1. Inform yourself

Bitcoin is different than what you know and use every day. Before you start using Bitcoin, there are a few things that you need to know in order to use it securely and avoid common pitfalls.

Read more

2. Choose your wallet

You can bring a Bitcoin wallet in your everyday life with your mobile or you can have a wallet only for online payments on your computer. In any case, choosing your wallet can be done in a minute.

Choose your wallet

3. Get Bitcoin

4. Spend Bitcoin

Our code

This is a somewhat simplified version of our `SpendMoney` function, which will handle someone who initiates a `Bitcoin.Spend` message. All you really need to do is supply the amount you want to spend, but, of course, this is far from production-ready code, so one of your exercises at the end of the chapter will be to widen this and the spend and receipt messages to fit your needs:

```
private void SpendMoney()
{
#region IMPORT PRIVKEY
var bitcoinPrivateKey = new
BitcoinSecret("cSZjE4aJNPpBtU6xvJ6J4iBzDgTmzTjbq8w2kqnYvAprBCyTsG4x");
var network = bitcoinPrivateKey.Network;
#endregion
var address = bitcoinPrivateKey.GetAddress();
var client = new QBitNinjaClient(network);
var transactionId =
uint256.Parse("e44587cf08b4f03b0e8b4ae7562217796ec47b8c91666681d71329b764ad
d2e3");
var transactionResponse = client.GetTransaction(transactionId)?.Result;var
receivedCoins = transactionResponse?.ReceivedCoins;OutPointoutPointToSpend
= null;
foreach (var coin in receivedCoins)
{
if (coin.TxOut?.ScriptPubKey == bitcoinPrivateKey.ScriptPubKey)
{
outPointToSpend = coin.Outpoint;
}
}
if (outPointToSpend== null)
throw new Exception("TxOut doesn't contain our ScriptPubKey");
var transaction = new Transaction();
transaction.Inputs?.Add(new TxIn()
{
PrevOut = outPointToSpend
});
var hallOfTheMakersAddress = new
BitcoinPubKeyAddress("mzp4No5cmCXjZUpf112B1XWsvWBfws5bbB");
// How much you want to TO
var hallOfTheMakersAmount = new Money((decimal) 0.5, MoneyUnit.BTC);
var minerFee = new Money((decimal) 0.0001, MoneyUnit.BTC);
// How much you want to spend FROM
var txInAmount = (Money) receivedCoins[(int) outPointToSpend.N]?.Amount;
Money changeBackAmount = txInAmount - hallOfTheMakersAmount - minerFee;
TxOut hallOfTheMakersTxOut = new TxOut()
```

```
{
Value = hallOfTheMakersAmount,
ScriptPubKey = hallOfTheMakersAddress.ScriptPubKey
};
TxOut changeBackTxOut = new TxOut()
{
Value = changeBackAmount,
ScriptPubKey = bitcoinPrivateKey.ScriptPubKey
};
transaction.Outputs?.Add(hallOfTheMakersTxOut);
transaction.Outputs?.Add(changeBackTxOut);
var message = "Our first bitcoin transaction together!";
var bytes = Encoding.UTF8.GetBytes(message);
transaction.Outputs?.Add(new TxOut()
{
Value = Money.Zero,
ScriptPubKey = TxNullDataTemplate.Instance?.GenerateScriptPubKey(bytes)
});
// It is also OK:
transaction.Inputs[0].ScriptSig = bitcoinPrivateKey.ScriptPubKey;
transaction.Sign(bitcoinPrivateKey, false);
BroadcastResponse broadcastResponse =
client.Broadcast(transaction)?.Result;
BitcoinSpendReceipt r = new BitcoinSpendReceipt();
if (!broadcastResponse.Success)
{
logger?.LogError($"ErrorCode: {broadcastResponse.Error.ErrorCode}");
logger?.LogError("Error message: " + broadcastResponse.Error.Reason);
r.success = false;
}
else
{
logger?.LogInformation("Success! You can check out the hash of the
transaction in any block explorer:");
logger?.LogInformation(transaction.GetHash()?.ToString());
r.success = true;
}
r.time = SystemClock.Instance.GetCurrentInstant().ToDateTimeUtc();
r.amount = txInAmount.ToDecimal(MoneyUnit.BTC);
Bus.Publish(r, "Bitcoin");
}
}
```

We've highlighted the portions of code that are used to publish the spend receipt message that everyone will be listening for. In a production-ready system, I could see a management role (microservice manager) that listens for the actual spending request message and approves or rejects it prior to sending it to the microservice.

Processing BitcoinSpendReceipt

Over in our microservice manager, it is sitting quietly just waiting to see whether we dared spend any money during this session. By subscribing to the BitcoinSpendReceipt message, once it arrives, we will know whether someone attempted to, or was successful in, spending our money and, if so, how much they spent. Here's our code to handle all that:

```
bool ProcessBitcoinSpendReceiptMessage(BitcoinSpendReceipt msg)\
 {
 Console.WriteLine("Received Bitcoin Spent Receipt");
 RILogManager.Default?.SendInformation("Received Bitcoin Spent Receipt
Message");
 if (msg.success)
 Console.WriteLine("Someone spent " + msg.amount + " of my bitcoins");
 else
 {
 Console.WriteLine("Someone tried to spend " + msg.amount + " of my
bitcoins");
 }
 return true;
 }
```

Summary

In this chapter, we exposed you to the very exciting cryptocurrency world of Bitcoin and blockchain. We helped you to develop a microservice that you can potentially leverage in a farm of many. We showed you several new and exciting open source packages, which we hope you will continue to find useful as the years go on. In the next chapter we will show you how you can quickly and easily add text to speech to your microservices and really make them exciting!

Exercises

1. Update the Bitcoin spending message to take multiple transactions
2. Work with other transactions and wallets

14
Adding Speech and Search to Your Microservice

In this chapter we are going to build an exciting, dual purpose microservice.

We will learn:

- How to use the Microsoft **Text-to-Speech** (**TTS**) engine
- How to build a microservice that can respond to speech requests
- How to use Text to Speech for search results

The internals are built around TTS specifically, the Microsoft Speech API. More concretely, we will use the TTS engine. Our microservice will be responsible for talking back to us, something I've always discouraged my children from ever doing to me, yet here I am programming a computer to do the same. But that's an entirely different book..

Our microservice will provide two unique pieces of functionality. First, you will be able to send a message and have the microservice repeat what you typed. You will have your choice of a male or female voice, the ability to set the volume and rate, and of course, the text. Just think of all the exciting things that you can do with this approach.

The second feature the microservice will implement is searching for a text term via Wikipedia. The results are then read to you via the text to speech engine.

Text-to-Speech

Starting back with Microsoft Windows Vista, the old **Speech Application Programming Interface** (**SAPI**) gained a new managed look. The `System.Speech` namespace allows developers to speech-enable applications. Here are the `System.Speech` namespaces available to you:

- `https://msdn.microsoft.com/en-us/library/system.speech.audioformat.aspx`
- `http://msdn2.microsoft.com/en-us/library/system.speech.recognition.aspx`
- `http://msdn2.microsoft.com/en-us/library/system.speech.recognition.aspx`
- `http://msdn2.microsoft.com/en-us/library/system.speech.synthesis.aspx`
- `http://msdn2.microsoft.com/en-us/library/system.speech.synthesis.ttsengine.aspx`

Not only does the TTS technology open the door to a significant portion of the population with literacy difficulties, learning disabilities, reduced vision, and language issues, but also to seniors and the broader online population (both young and old) who are looking for convenient ways to access content:

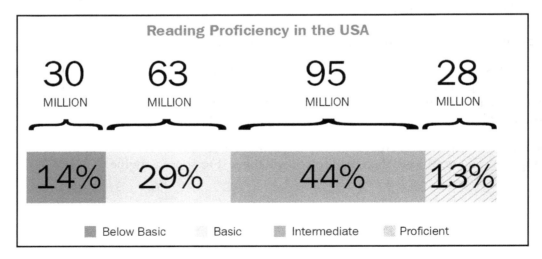

It is absolutely mind-boggling that 15-20% of the population worldwide has some form of language-based learning disability. This is just one of the many areas where TTS can prove its value. Add to that the alarming rate of high school students who graduate yet read at a very low-grade level, and you have a huge value add that TTS can provide. And don't forget that the language-based disability is worldwide, meaning it's not just in English. By being able to support multiple languages we add a huge value in any situation.

Another aspect of assistance our approach takes is addressing the ever-growing population of senior citizens around the world that are just now coming into the digital age:

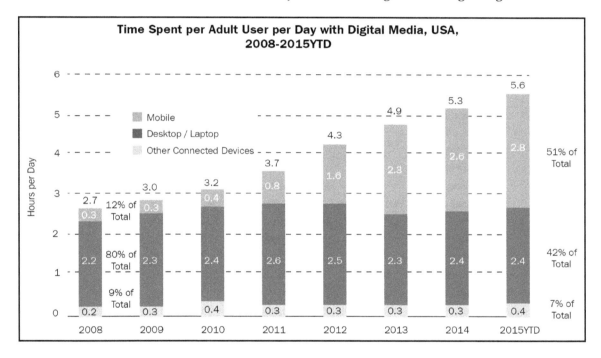

For senior citizens, the digital age can be very frightening. You go from 50 years of having paper bank statements to now having it available in this thing called the Cloud, which no one can quantify. From getting a check in the mail each month to now just trusting that it's in the bank, from writing checks to pushing buttons. From driving to see the grandchildren once a year to FaceTiming them every weekend. Hopefully, you can see that not only has the number of people accessing digital media increased, but for some it's not been as enjoyable or stress free as it has for many others. So, TTS makes this transition into the digital age a bit less user hostile.

Our next screenshot also helps us determine how important a smooth transition to digital media can be. The following chart shows the average time spent per day on major media by US adults:

Share of Average Time Spent per Day with Major Media by US Adults, 2014-2019 % of total	2014	2015	2016	2017	2018	2019
Digital	42.9%	45.3%	47.2%	48.9%	50.4%	51.6%
—Mobile (nonvoice)	21.6%	23.9%	25.7%	27.3%	28.6%	29.6%
——Audio	5.8%	6.6%	7.1%	7.3%	7.5%	7.6%
——Social networks	3.2%	3.9%	4.8%	5.6%	6.0%	6.4%
——Video*	3.0%	3.6%	4.2%	4.6%	5.0%	5.3%
——Other	9.5%	9.7%	9.7%	9.8%	10.1%	10.3%
—Desktop/laptop**	18.6%	18.2%	17.4%	17.0%	16.8%	16.7%
——Audio	0.9%	0.9%	0.9%	0.8%	0.8%	0.7%
——Video*	3.3%	3.4%	3.4%	3.4%	3.3%	3.3%
——Social networks	1.9%	1.7%	1.5%	1.5%	1.4%	1.4%
——Other	12.6%	12.2%	11.7%	11.4%	11.3%	11.3%
—Other connected devices	2.7%	3.2%	4.0%	4.6%	5.0%	5.3%
TV***		36.6%	35.1%	34.1%	33.0%	32.0%	31.2%
Radio***		12.4%	12.3%	12.0%	11.9%	11.8%	11.7%
Print***	4.4%	4.0%	3.5%	3.3%	3.1%	3.0%
——Newspapers	2.6%	2.3%	2.0%	1.8%	1.7%	1.6%
——Magazines	1.9%	1.7%	1.5%	1.5%	1.4%	1.3%
Other***	3.6%	3.4%	3.1%	2.9%	2.7%	2.6%

Note: ages 18+; time spent with each medium includes all time spent with that medium, regardless of multitasking; for example, 1 hour of multitasking on desktop/laptop while watching TV is counted as 1 hour for TV and 1 hour for desktop/laptop; numbers may not add up to 100% due to rounding; *excludes time spent with video via social networks; **includes all internet activities on desktop and laptop computers; ***excludes digital Source: eMarketer, Sep 2017

Installation

As always, we will create a .NET Framework console application, and we will name it `SpeechBotMicroService` as follows:

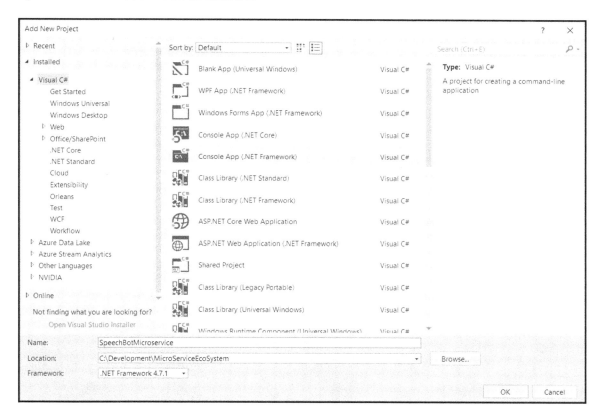

Our program

Here is a look at our `Main` function, completely filled out. We register our types and interfaces, build the `Autofac` container, and configure and then run the microservice. We also configured the microservice with leadership ability as seen in earlier chapters, in case you decide to run multiple instances of the microservice. Wow, that would be chatty, wouldn't it?:

```
static void Main(string[] args)
{
```

```
var builder = new ContainerBuilder();
// Service itself
builder.RegisterType<MSBaseLogger>()?.SingleInstance();
builder.RegisterType<SpeechBot>()
.AsImplementedInterfaces()
.AsSelf()
?.InstancePerLifetimeScope();
_container = builder.Build();
XmlConfigurator.ConfigureAndWatch(new FileInfo(@".log4net.config"));
HostFactory.Run(c =>
{
c?.UseAutofacContainer(_container);
c?.UseLog4Net();
c?.ApplyCommandLineWithDebuggerSupport();
c?.EnablePauseAndContinue();
c?.EnableShutdown();
c?.OnException(ex => Console.WriteLine(ex.Message));
c?.UseWindowsHostEnvironmentWithDebugSupport();
c?.Service<SpeechBot>(s =>
{
s.ConstructUsingAutofacContainer<SpeechBot>();
s?.ConstructUsing(settings =>
{
var service =
AutofacHostBuilderConfigurator.LifetimeScope.Resolve<SpeechBot>();
return service;
});
s?.ConstructUsing(name => new SpeechBot(_container,
Guid.NewGuid().ToString()));

// The following code block handles leader management for multi-instance
microservices
s?.WhenStartedAsLeader(b =>
{
b.WhenStarted(async (service, token) =>
{
await service.Start(token);
});
b.Lease(lcb => lcb.RenewLeaseEvery(TimeSpan.FromSeconds(2))
.AquireLeaseEvery(TimeSpan.FromSeconds(5))
.LeaseLength(TimeSpan.FromDays(1))
.WithLeaseManager(new SpeechBot()));
b.WithHeartBeat(TimeSpan.FromSeconds(30), (isLeader, token) =>
Task.CompletedTask);
b.Build();
});
//
```

```
s?.WhenStarted((SpeechBot server, HostControl host) =>
server.OnStart(host));
s?.WhenPaused(server => server?.OnPause());
s?.WhenContinued(server => server?.OnResume());
s?.WhenStopped(server => server?.OnStop());
s?.WhenShutdown(server => server?.OnShutdown());
s?.WhenCustomCommandReceived((server, host, code) => { });
s?.AfterStartingService(() => { });
s?.AfterStoppingService(() => { });
s?.BeforeStartingService(() => { });
s?.BeforeStoppingService(() => { });
});
c?.RunAsNetworkService();
c?.StartAutomaticallyDelayed();
c?.SetDescription(string.Intern("Speech Bot Microservice"));
c?.SetDisplayName(string.Intern("SpeechBotMicroservice"));
c?.SetServiceName(string.Intern("SpeechBotMicroservice"));
c?.EnableServiceRecovery(r =>
{
r?.OnCrashOnly();
r?.RestartService(1); //first
r?.RestartService(1); //second
r?.RestartService(1); //subsequents
r?.SetResetPeriod(0);
});
});
}
```

Our messages

For this microservice, we are choosing to not have reply messages. There's nothing saying any one way is better than the other. If you believe that you need response messages in order to validate the chain of custody or just to log compliance, then feel free to create a message, register it, subscribe, and process it accordingly. For our purposes we will simply send requests and assume they were processed.

The first message is for our Wikipedia search. The second message is for our text to speech translation:

```
[Queue("Speech", ExchangeName = "EvolvedAI")]
[Serializable]
public class WikipediaSearchMessage
{
public int maxReturns { get; set; }
public string searchTerm { get; set; }
```

```
}
[Queue("Speech", ExchangeName = "EvolvedAI")]
[Serializable]
public class SpeechRequestMessage
{
public int ID { get; set; }
public string text { get; set; }
public int maleSpeaker { get; set; }
public int volume { get; set; }
public int rate { get; set; }
}
```

Subscribing to messages

In order to receive messages we have to subscribe to them. Similar to what we have done in earlier chapters of the book, here we are subscribing to our Speech queue on the EvolvedAI exchange. We will be looking for any messages with the topic of Speech:

```
private void Subscribe()
{
Bus = RabbitHutch.CreateBus("host=localhost",
x =>
{
x.Register<IConventions, AttributeBasedConventions>();
x.EnableMessageVersioning();
});
IExchange exchange = Bus?.Advanced?.ExchangeDeclare("EvolvedAI",
ExchangeType.Topic);
IQueue queue = Bus?.Advanced?.QueueDeclare("Speech");
Bus?.Advanced?.Bind(exchange, queue, "");
Bus?.Subscribe<SpeechRequestMessage>(Environment.MachineName, msg =>
ProcessSpeechRequestMessage(msg),
config => config?.WithTopic("Speech"));
Bus?.Subscribe<WikipediaSearchMessage>(Environment.MachineName, msg =>
ProcessWikipediaSearchMessage(msg),
config => config?.WithTopic("Speech"));
}
```

Processing speech request messages

Once we receive a message, specifically a speech request message, we need to process it. This message is telling us to use the text to speech engine to repeat vocally what was presented to us as text. We will assume that the validity of the message contents was checked on the sending side.

First, we will set the voice to be male or female, based upon the `maleSpeaker` flag in the message. We then set the volume and rate, pass in the text of the message, and let the TTS engine play back the audio:

```
bool ProcessSpeechRequestMessage(SpeechRequestMessage msg)
{
WriteLineInColor("Received Speech Bot Request", ConsoleColor.Red);
WriteLineInColor("Text to speak: " + msg.text, ConsoleColor.Yellow);
voice?.SelectVoiceByHints(msg.maleSpeaker == 1 ? VoiceGender.Male :
VoiceGender.Female);
Ensure.Argument(msg.volume).GreaterThanOrEqualTo(0);
Ensure.Argument(msg.volume).LessThanOrEqualTo(100);
Ensure.Argument(msg.rate).GreaterThanOrEqualTo(-10);
Ensure.Argument(msg.rate).LessThanOrEqualTo(10);
voice.Volume = msg.volume;
voice.Rate = msg.rate;
PromptBuilder builder = new PromptBuilder();
builder.ClearContent();
builder.StartSentence();
builder.AppendText(msg?.text);
builder.EndSentence();
voice.SpeakAsync(builder);
return true;
}
```

The `volume` number ranges from zero to one hundred inclusive, where `100` is the maximum value and `0` is the minimum.

The `rate` number ranges from -10 to 10. A value of zero sets the voice to talk at its default pitch. A value of -10 sets the voice to speak at one-third of its default rate. A value of 10 sets the voice to speak at three times its default rate. Values outside this range will be passed to the TTS engine; however, the operating characteristics are undefined and vary by the voice. Each increment between -10 and 10 is logarithmically distributed such that incrementing or decrementing by one is multiplying or dividing the rate by the *10th* root of three (about *1.1*). Values more extreme than -10 and 10 will be passed to an engine. However, TTS engines that comply with the speech platform may not support such extremes and may clip the rate to the maximum or minimum rate the engine supports.

The TTS API offers two events that we need to subscribe to. They are `SpeakStarted` and `SpeakCompleted`. Once we execute the `voice.SpeakAsync` call, the `SpeakStarted` event will be fired. Once speaking is complete, the `SpeakCompleted` event will be fired. You can use these two events to track when your microservice is speaking. We could send status messages to make sure that other people do not send us requests until we are capable of responding. The other usage for these events is internal to our microservice, in that we could show and hide our dialog screen, and many other things. For the purposes of this demonstration, we will just set a Boolean flag to indicate whether or not we are actually speaking at the moment:

```
private bool speaking;
private void Voice_SpeakStarted(object sender, SpeakStartedEventArgs e)
{
speaking = true;
}
private void Voice_SpeakCompleted(object sender, SpeakCompletedEventArgs e)
{
speaking = false;
}
```

Processing Wikipedia search messages

The second function of our microservice is to conduct a search of a specific term on Wikipedia. In order to do this we are using the Wikipedia open source library found on GitHub. At the time of the writing of this book a NuGet package was not available so the source was downloaded and compiled. Both the source and the compiled binary are available via the website information listed in the front of the book. The function will look like this:

```
bool ProcessWikipediaSearchMessage(WikipediaSearchMessage msg)
{
SearchWikipedia(msg.searchTerm, msg.maxReturns, msg.maxReturns,
```

```
Language.English);
return true;
}
```

Why search Wikipedia? Why not, **Alexa** does, right? So you now will have the capability to perform searches for things and have their results spoken back to you. You might be wanting to learn the definition of a word, understand what a new term means, or perhaps you just like the sound of synthesized voices. You might also be one of the many people that suffer from learning disabilities to the extent that having the text spoken to you would be a huge benefit.

Our `SearchWikipedia` function takes in the search term, the maximum number of results we will allow back, the maximum number of events we wish read back to us, and the language. Our API supports all 283 languages of the Wikipedia site:

If no results are found then the TTS engine will say that to us, otherwise, the results will be spoken to us until the maximum number of responses is reached:

```
private void SearchWikipedia(string text, int maxResults, int
resultsToRead)
{
wikipedia.Limit = maxResults;
voice.SpeakAsync("I just received a search request for the term " + text);
QueryResult results = wikipedia.Search(text);
if (results.Search.Count == 0)
{
voice.SpeakAsync("I'm sorry, I could not find anything for " + text);
}
else
{
if (results.Search.Count < resultsToRead)
```

```
resultsToRead = results.Search.Count;
voice.SpeakAsync("I found " + results.Search.Count +
" results for " + text + ". According to Wikipedia, here are the top " +
resultsToRead + " results I found");
PromptBuilder builder = new PromptBuilder();
builder.StartSentence();
for (intx = 0; x < resultsToRead; x++)
{
builder.AppendText(results.Search[x].Snippet.Substring(
results.Search[x].Snippet.LastIndexOf("</span>") + 7));
}
builder.EndSentence();
voice.SpeakAsync(builder);
}
}
```

Using Text-to-Speech

The following is an example of our `SpeechRequestMessage` that we are sending to the TTS engine. The rate is an integral value between –10 and 10, the volume is an integral value between 0 and 100, and the `maleSpeaker` parameter is either one for a male voice, or zero for a female voice.

We arranged for quite a lot of text to be spoken so that you have enough text to get a feel for the benefits of TTS. Please feel free to customize the text to whatever works best for your situation:

```
SpeechRequestMessage msg = new SpeechRequestMessage
{
rate = 0,
maleSpeaker = 0,
volume = 50,
ID = 1,
text =
"As to country N and President Z, we believe we're entering a missile
renaissance, said Ian Williams, ",
};
```

msg.text += " an associate director at the center for strategic and International Studies, who has been compiling data on missile programs in different countries.";

msg.text += " A growing number of countries with ready access to missiles increases regional tensions and makes war more likely, Mr.Williams said. Countries are more apt to use their arsenals if they think their missiles could be targeted.";

msg.text += " In addition, many of the missiles being developed by these countries are based on obsolete technologies, which makes them less accurate, increasing the risk to civilians. And there is a risk that missiles could fall into the hands of militias and terrorist groups.";

msg.text += " Y'all should buy Bitcoin at $15543. Foreign currency comes in at ? 12435. It might also show, says Mr. Williams, like ? 15533435.";

```
Bus.Publish(msg, "Speech");
```

I should also point out to you that what we are doing is no different than the **Read Aloud** functionality that Microsoft has added to several of their Microsoft Office Suite of products, including Microsoft Word and Microsoft Outlook, as shown in the following screenshot:

Microsoft Word read aloud:

Microsoft Outlook read aloud:

Summary

In this chapter we showed you how to add text to speech to a microservice By supporting regular TTS requests as well as speaking the results of a Wikipedia search, we showed you the many benefits of using TTS. We also showed how what we are doing is similar to the functionality that Microsoft has added to its Microsoft Office suite of products. Offering this capability in a microservice opens a world of opportunities for those who choose to approach it with an open mind. Just think about all the places where you have text or documents that need to be proofread, verified, or just read aloud.

As we have come to the end of this book I want to extend a huge thank you to those who have read and/or purchased this book. I hope that you open your mind to how a huge microservice ecosystem could be built, and that you will take what we have learned and extend it into new and fascinating approaches. I would love to see the projects you end up with. Feel free to contact me through the contact information in the front of the book.

Best Practices

In this chapter, we are going to discuss best practices for designing and using your microservice ecosystem. Although I am going to provide you with some best practices that I have in mind, feel free to update this as you see fit. Also keep in mind that, as C# developers, we realize that we don't always have a choice or preference in this. Even though it's our best practice, it might not be our team or our company's best practice. A good example would be that your databases have probably been in place a long time and the database administrators probably are not overly sensitive to our architectural preferences. In the end, you'll have to make the call on each one of the recommendations listed. Just do your best and think it through. Some will apply, some you won't be allowed to do, that's just the nature of how we do what we do!

Microservices

- Each microservice should be developed and deployed independently.
- There should be no dependency between your microservice, or any other microservice or application, if possible.
- Your microservice should be deployable all by itself.
- Each microservice should be its own solution/codebase.
- Each microservice should have its own data sources. Now, while this is the accepted best practice, it doesn't always hold up. If your project is a green-field project, perhaps you will get lucky, otherwise, we usually have data sources developed and in use long before we get to this project. Although a best practice, it is often not applicable for various reasons.
- Each microservice should communicate with other microservices via an asynchronous, event-driven, message-based approach to reduce inter-service dependencies.
- The change of one microservice should not break another. This sometimes does happen, but we should try to minimize such an occurrence.
- Each microservice should be small enough to serve a specific business purpose, yet big enough to minimize any inter-service dependencies.
- Never wait to return from processing a message. Spawn a background working process.

- Always use the *Hollywood Principle*. What does that mean? *Don't call us, we'll call you!* In microservice speak, that means don't poll for information, just wait for messages to arrive!

- Use circuit breaker patterns wherever possible. A circuit-breaker prevents requests that are known to fail (usually to a previous failure attempt) from being attempted. If there are failures, set a flag and stop trying for a designated period. Once that time has expired, reset the flag and try again. The status of your circuit breaker should be reported to the health monitoring microservice. I also recommend what is known as **exponential backoff** for your circuit-breaker. What this means is that each subsequent request for something that previously failed is spread out a bit longer than the previous request. This gives the error condition more time to heal itself. If the first retry was done after 10 seconds, the second could be done after 15, the third after 20, and so on.

- Message sending and receive should be done asynchronously.

- User correlation IDs. The chain of custody in a microservice is so very important. Being able to trace a complete event history from start to finish is invaluable, and passing a chain of custody identifier (correlation ID) is the way to handle this. When you are trying to resurrect the complete path of a request or event, this will help you to do so.

- Your microservice should be stateless if running behind a load balancer. Having a state-based microservice can be very beneficial if done correctly. Just remember that this could have a negative impact if running behind a load balancer.

- Think carefully about how your microservice will function if one or more microservices, services, or applications are down or encounter errors.

- Each microservice should have automated monitoring and alerting in case of problems. Agree on what it means for a microservice to be in an unhealthy state, what an alert will do, mean, and provide, and implement accordingly.

- Always have a second-level microservice designed for nothing but health-monitoring.

- Understand how decentralized interactions benefit you. Each microservice must take full responsibility for its role in the greater ecosystem. Each microservice must listen for events and messages, complete all work as quickly as possible, make sure that a retry mechanism exists for handling failures, and send result messages quickly if required. Doing so will give us loose coupling and high cohesion, resulting in greater autonomy for each microservice and your ecosystem. This is another reason to have a health monitor microservice: so as to be able to track statuses, events, and so on.

- Strive for separation of concerns whenever possible.

- Strive for idempotency. Jobs or tasks should be able to be retried multiple times.
- Strive for eventual consistency. In short, this means that if no new request has been made to the microservice, once a request is made, it will return the last updated data or item.
- Use asynchronous workers whenever possible. Why?
    - This speeds up the request path as requests are non-blocking.
    - This spreads the load to allow for easier scalability.
    - This reduces errors since failed workers can be retried behind the scenes.

Messaging

- Keep your message queues as short as possible. Many messages in a queue can put a heavy load on RAM usage. When this happens, RabbitMQ will start flushing messages to disk to free up RAM, and when that happens, queuing speeds will deteriorate. This paging process can take some time and will block the queue from processing messages. When there are a lot of messages to page out, it can take considerable time and will affect the performance of the broker negatively.
- Limit the number of messaging queues that you have. Queues are single-threaded in RabbitMQ, and one queue can handle up to about 50,000 messages. You will achieve better throughput on a multi-core system if you have multiple queues and consumers. You will achieve optimal throughput if you have as many queues as cores on the underlying node(s).
- Split your messaging queues over multiple cores. Queue performance is limited to one CPU core. You will, therefore, get better performance if you split your queues into different cores, and into different nodes if you have a RabbitMQ cluster.
- If you cannot afford to lose any messages, make sure that your messaging queue is declared as durable and your messages are sent with the persistent delivery mode.

Scheduling jobs

- In-progress jobs marked **recoverable** are automatically re-executed after a scheduler fails. This means some of the job's **work** will be executed twice, so the job should be coded in such a way that its work is idempotent.
- Avoid scheduling any jobs during the **Daylight Savings Time** (**DST**) interval. **SimpleTriggers** are not affected by DST as they always fire at an exact millisecond in time and repeat an exact number of milliseconds apart. Because **CronTriggers** fire at given hours/minutes/seconds, they are subject to some oddities when DST transitions occur.

As an example of possible issues, when scheduling in the United States within time zones /locations that observe DST, the following problems may occur if using CronTrigger and scheduling fire times from 1:00 AM to 2:00 AM:

- 1:05 AM may occur twice–duplicate firings on CronTrigger possible
- 2:05 AM may never occur–missed firings on CronTrigger possible

Recommended reading

These suggestions have nothing to do with microservice development *per se*, but are books I recommend you read in order to become a better all-around developer:

- *How to Lie with Statistics* by Darrell Huff. This is an old book, very small, but it does an excellent job explaining how one statistic can be used in several different manners, all with the correct meaning. It also tells you that 84.5% of all statistics used are false. By the way, I just made that number up as well. The moral here is always investigate, study, and understand for yourself. If someone throws a statistic at you, such as RabbitMQ percentages or the number of microservices developed in Java versus C#, always verify what you hear.
- The *Death of Expertise* by Tom Nichols. Trust me on this one!
- *Hands-On Machine Learning in C#* by me. Shameless plug, but hey, I'm the author, right?

Index

www.ingramcontent.com/pod-product-compliance
Lightning Source LLC
Chambersburg PA
CBHW080636060326
40690CB00021B/4953

* 9 7 8 1 7 8 9 5 3 3 6 8 2 *